WE SPEAK BECAUSE WE HAVE
FIRST BEEN SPOKEN

We Speak Because We Have First Been Spoken

A Grammar of the Preaching Life

Michael Pasquarello III

WILLIAM B. EERDMANS PUBLISHING COMPANY

GRAND RAPIDS, MICHIGAN / CAMBRIDGE, U.K.

Published 2009 by
Wm. B. Eerdmans Publishing Co.
2140 Oak Industrial Drive N.E., Grand Rapids, Michigan 49505 /
P.O. Box 163, Cambridge CB3 9PU U.K.

Printed in the United States of America

14 13 12 11 10 09   7 6 5 4 3 2 1

Library of Congress Cataloging-in-Publication Data

Pasquarello, Michael.
We speak because we have first been spoken:
a grammar of the preaching life / Michael Pasquarello III.
p.   cm.
Includes bibliographical references.
ISBN 978-0-8028-2917-7 (pbk.: alk. paper)
1. Preaching.   I. Title.

BV4211.3.P366   2009
251 — dc22

2009029274

www.eerdmans.com

Contents

Preface

I WANT TO thank Mr. Sam Eerdmans and the staff of the William B. Eerdmans Publishing Company for their enthusiastic support of this project from the time it was first proposed. It is a joy to write for a publisher that is deeply committed to engaging serious theological matters. This is especially encouraging for those who work in the field of homiletics and who have watched preaching in many congregations during the past generation be reduced to "how to" techniques that are judged on the basis of "effectiveness," which is typically measured in culturally defined, quantitative terms. The person of the preacher is now a mere technician, a "communicator," whose task is to produce results, rather than a truthful witness to the wisdom and virtue of the incarnate Word, whom we are called to follow and proclaim as the source and end of things.

The aim of this book is to provide a vision that reunites the life of the preacher with the content and activity of preaching — the "preaching life" — within the wisdom of the triune God and the life of the church as Christ's body. It contributes to overcoming the Creator/creation, sacred/secular, theology/practice, Word/flesh dualism, what Charles Taylor describes as the "excarnation," which long predates its recent popular and more sophisticated manifestations in North America among evangelical, mainline, and emergent churches.

I am most grateful to a number of audiences who have been receptive to this subject in presentations I have made during the past several years: my "Theology and Practice of Preaching" classes at Asbury Theological Seminary; my doctor of ministry advisees and students at Asbury; the Salvation Army Continuing Education preaching course and Homiletic Symposium; pastors at the Calvin Seminary Symposium on Worship; the "History of Preaching" group at the Academy of Homiletics; and members of the Oxford Institute for Methodist Theological Studies. Their questions and suggestions have helped to stimulate and clarify my thinking.

As a member of the Wesleyan tradition, I have been prompted in my thinking on this subject by my ongoing conversation with John Wesley, who once wrote, "I do indeed live by preaching."[1] My intention has been to live more fully into the vocation of "preacher" and to understand more clearly its "grammar" by reflecting on what it might mean to confess with Wesley, in our time, "I do indeed live by preaching." Because it was not possible for Wesley to conceive of the calling to preach apart from the person who preaches, or to think of preaching "scriptural holiness" without faith energized by love suffusing the preacher's whole manner of living and speaking, I want to suggest that it might be equally fitting to say, "I do indeed preach by living."

The poet Wendell Berry says, "We are speaking where we stand, and we shall stand afterwards in the presence of what we have said."[2] *We Speak Because We Have First Been Spoken* is dedicated to friends and colleagues in the "preaching life" whose desire is to live and speak well, since in the end they will be one — when words and deeds, words and things, and words and people stand in fidelity to one another in the presence of the one by whom all things have been spoken. St. Augustine affirms this truth eloquently:

> The reward of virtue will be God himself, who gave the virtue, together with the promise of himself, the best and greatest of all possible promises. For what did he mean when he said, in the words of the prophet, "I shall be their God, and they will be my people . . . ?" He will be the goal of all our longings; and we shall see him forever; we shall love him without satiety; we shall praise him without wearying. This will be the duty, the delight, the activity of all, shared by all who

1. Cited in Albert C. Outler, ed., "Introduction," *The Works of John Wesley,* vol. I, *Sermons,* Bicentennial Edition (Nashville: Abingdon, 1984), 13.

2. Wendell Berry, *Standing by Words* (Washington, DC: Shoemaker and Hoard, 1983), 62.

share the life of eternity. . . . Nothing will give more joy to that City than this song to the glory of Christ by whose blood we have been set free. There the precept will find fulfillment: "Be still, and know that I am God."[3]

Finally, I wish to thank my wife, Patti, whose love, friendship, and encouragement have meant so much as I have slowly brought this project to completion. She continually reminds me that such work is an occasion for joy. Thanks be to God.

Easter, 2008

---

3. Augustine, *Concerning the City of God: Against the Pagans,* trans. Henry Bettenson, ed. David Knowles (New York: Pelican Books, 1974), XXII.30.

Introduction:
We Speak Because We Have First Been Spoken

THE IDEA for this book has developed during more than twenty-five years of preaching and conversing with church members, preachers, seminarians, teachers of preaching, and sermon listeners in general concerning our contemporary homiletical situation in North America. Many of these conversations have pointed to a need for clarity about the character of "preacher" for a postliberal, post-Christendom church,[1] which I would describe in the following way: an exemplary witness whose way of living and speaking the gospel — the call to holiness of life communicated by Jesus Christ — is formed by prayerful attentiveness

---

1. What I am referring to as "Christendom" is developed in the Gifford Lectures of Stanley Hauerwas, who writes of modernity's temptation to cast Christianity as a truth separate from truthful witness: "At least one name for this temptation is 'Constantinianism.' As a result of the attempt to make Christianity anyone's fate, the truth is that God is assumed to be available to anyone, without moral transformation and spiritual guidance." Stanley Hauerwas, *With the Grain of the Universe: The Church's Witness and Natural Theology* (Grand Rapids: Brazos, 2001), 36 and passim. For recent thinking on "postliberalism," see Robert Barron, *The Priority of Christ: Toward a Postliberal Catholicism* (Grand Rapids: Brazos, 2007), 13. "[L]iberal modernity can best be seen as an energetic reaction to a particular and problematic version of nominalist Christianity. Early modernity saw itself as a salutary response to oppressive and obscurantist strains in Christian culture, but since it was reacting to a corruption of true Christianity, it itself became similarly distorted and exaggerated." I suspect this kind of "liberalism" is pervasive among both mainline and evangelical churches, "packaged" in a variety of political/cultural expressions of "Christendom," which tend to reduce divine revelation to personal religious experience.

to, and participation in, the communion of love enjoyed by the Father and the Son in the Spirit.[2]

Writing in the first handbook for preachers, St. Augustine concludes that nothing is more important for a preacher than to become "a living sermon," a person whose language and life are becoming one with the truth of God incarnate in Christ.[3] Yet only the inexhaustibly generous self-communication of the triune God, the Father and the Son in the Spirit, is capable of elevating and renewing our human capacities for homiletical excellence that is evinced by keen intellect, deep piety, holy living, and virtuous speech. Moreover, as Robert Barron notes, such participatory knowing will embrace one's whole being — body, will, mind, and heart — and requires attentiveness, intelligence, reasonableness, and responsibility, which, by the work of divine grace, draws us out of ourselves and conforms us to the truth of God and his plan for salvation in Christ and the church.[4]

These three elements will be essential for discussing a "grammar of the preaching life": attention/contemplation, the integration of theology and practice, and communion/participation. This book argues that the modern functional divide between theology and preaching is overcome by the attentiveness of faith in the incarnate Word through the grace of the Spirit, who transforms a preacher to participate in the truth and goodness of the one who is proclaimed. As Craig Dykstra explains, "Language and action cannot be separated. . . . The way of living deepens the understanding of the language, while a deepening understanding of the language enables new levels of participation in the way of living."[5] Joe Jones puts it this way: "The deepest form of truth in Christian

---

2. Robert W. Jenson says: "As the church speaks and hears the gospel and as the church responds in prayer and confession, the church's life is a great conversation, and this conversation is none other than our anticipatory participation in the converse of the Father and the Son in the Spirit; as the church is enlivened and empowered by this hearing and answer, the inspiration is none other than the Spirit who is the life between the Father and the Son." Jenson, *Systematic Theology: The Triune God*, vol. 1 (Oxford: Oxford University Press, 1997), 228.

3. Augustine, *Teaching Christianity* [De Doctrina Christiana], in *The Works of Saint Augustine, a Translation of the 21st Century*, trans. Edmund Hill, O.P. (Hyde Park, NY: New City Press, 1996), IV. 61.

4. Barron, *The Priority of Christ*, 170.

5. Craig Dykstra, *Growing in the Life of Faith: Education and Christian Practices*, 2nd ed. (Louisville: Westminster John Knox, 2005), 126.

discourses and practices is a life in intentional conformity to the triune Life of God. . . . This is to embody the truth of Jesus Christ."[6]

What we need is not a new and more relevant method, technique, or way of preaching; rather, we need intellectual and moral habits that enable us to discern how to love wisely and speak well according to God's providential wisdom, which finds its center in the Word by which the world was made and the incarnate Word by which the world is re-made, the "economy for the fullness of times, to recapitulate all things in Christ, things in heaven and things on earth" (Eph. 1:10).[7]

In a discussion of early Christian thought, Robert Wilken observes that authority has to do with the quality of a person's life as a truthful, trustworthy witness, and that trusting in authority is a necessary part of the knowledge that is received by faith. However, he adds: "This is not primarily a matter of gaining information, but involves habits, attitudes, and dispositions that have to do with one's loves. This kind of knowledge, the knowledge one lives by, is gained gradually over time. . . . The knowledge of God sinks into the mind and heart slowly and hence requires apprenticeship."[8]

We cannot reason our way to God without entrusting ourselves to others who know and love God. The things that matter — God, humanity, and the world — are not learned without sympathy and enthusiasm, without our giving of ourselves, without a debt of love. The place where we must begin is with the persons whose lives are formed by the teaching, since Christian witness is inescapably bound to the witness of others, to a kind of seeing, or knowing, that is faith. "There is no way to Christ without *martyrs,* without witnesses."[9]

For this reason, the most important element of sermon prepara-

---

6. Joe R, Jones, *A Grammar of Christian Faith: Systematic Explorations in Christian Life and Doctrine* (Lanham, MD: Rowman & Littlefield Publishers, 2002), 1:109. Jones describes the grammar of God's self-revelation in Jesus Christ: "The confession that the church speaks because God has first spoken and revealed Godself is fundamental to Christian witness and self-understanding" (p. 79). I am indebted to Jones's work in my thinking about these matters.

7. See John J. O' Keefe and R. R. Reno, *Sanctified Vision: An Introduction to Early Christian Interpretation of the Bible* (Baltimore: Johns Hopkins University Press, 2005).

8. Robert Louis Wilken, *The Spirit of Early Christian Thought: Seeking the Face of God* (New Haven: Yale University Press, 2003), 172.

9. Wilken, *The Spirit of Early Christian Thought,* 173, 180.

tion is the *theological, spiritual, and moral formation* of the preacher through the Spirit's empowerments of faith, hope, and love, which are completed by the gifts of wisdom, understanding, counsel, strength, knowledge, godliness, and fear of the Lord (Isa. 11). Learning the "grammar" of the preaching life requires cultivating habits of the mind, heart, and body — including speaking truthfully — that are intrinsic to the church's vocation of knowing and worshiping the triune God. If this is true, preaching excellence will be the fruit of listening to God's prior Word and act before we ourselves presume to speak. And because the depth and riches of God's Word are too great to absorb in a lifetime, we will have cause to listen for eternity. [10]

Learning the grammar of the preaching life is inseparable from the holiness of life that is shaped by schooling in prayer as the practice of love, which leads to the knowledge of God.[11] Knowing God comprises a depth of personal acquaintance, delight in appreciating the other, and desire for deeper understanding or "desiring God and learning in love."[12] Moreover, love's knowledge is a good in itself, an integrative activity that orders us to loving contemplation and joyful proclamation of what is supremely beautiful and good. In other words, prayer is the movement of the heart toward God, and is the response of the heart to God's self-giving love in Jesus Christ. In addition, prayer is engagement with the object of our faith, an object that is in some way apprehended or known in a cognitive engagement involving the mind: faith as thinking with assent that is penetrated by love.[13] In an essay on the theology

10. Stanley Hauerwas speaks of the careful attention we must give to how we speak in order to be faithful witnesses by what we speak: "For the testing of Christian speech is prayer. The decisive form of prayer is the liturgy in which the sermon is one of the central acts of praise. The Church's doctrinal debates are rightly about how we are to pray so that our words do not betray the one to whom we pray." Hauerwas, "Foreword," in *Heresies and How to Avoid Them: Why It Matters What Christians Believe,* ed. Ben Quash and Michael Ward (Peabody, MA: Hendrickson, 2007), x.

11. See the excellent discussion in Gavin D'Costa, *Theology in the Public Square: Church, Academy and Nation* (Oxford: Blackwell, 2005), 138; cf. chap. 4, "Why Theologians Must Pray for Release from Exile."

12. See the excellent development of this theme in David F. Ford, *Christian Wisdom: Desiring God and Learning in Love* (Cambridge, UK: Cambridge University Press, 2007).

13. For this understanding of prayer, I am indebted to Andrew Louth, *Discerning the Mystery: An Essay on the Nature of Theology* (Oxford: Clarendon Press, 1983), 3.

of Thomas Aquinas, A. N. Williams describes how theology, prayer, worship, and the Christian life are integrally related in contemplating God and the things of God:

> It is concerned with the transformative possibilities of the contemplation of God: how the believer may not only assent to the propositions of faith but may be joined to God through faith.... One contemplates, not in order to make God welcome where he would otherwise not be, but in order to make oneself present before the face of transforming glory. The communal and communicative dimension of theology does not disappear, but becomes the consequence of spiritual formation. We do not speak in order that others will be persuaded; we speak because we have been transformed.[14]

Knowing and loving God engenders the capacity for theological judgment as well as the habits of vision and discernment that form a preacher to "speak Christian" according to "the grammar of Christ."[15]

In this book I argue for a recovery of the "preaching life," which integrates the person *and* work of the preacher through participation in the "grammar" of Christ, who ". . . at every turn and in every detail [is] the grammar, syntax, and vocabulary that God uses to tell his own story."[16] As recipients of the Father's self-giving through the missions of the Son and Spirit, we have been made participants in a Trinitarian pedagogy that reorders our desire to know and love God, and thus, to fully be.[17]

---

14. A. N. Williams, "Mystical Theology Redux: The Pattern of Aquinas' *Summa Theologiae*," *Modern Theology* 13, no. 1 (Jan. 1997): 69.

15. Charles M. Wood, *Vision and Discernment: An Orientation in Theological Study* (Atlanta: Scholars Press, 1995). "The educational use of theological inquiry also involves the making of theological judgments, and also has a practical intention; but its more proper aim is not the formation of judgments, but the formation of judgment. Its impact upon Christian practice is indirect. It informs practice by equipping the practitioner not with ready-made deliberative judgments but rather with the capacity to make them. . . . [L]earning to exercise these capacities, learning theological judgment, learning to discern and envision, is indeed a kind of personal formation" (pp. 80, 88).

16. Barron, *The Priority of Christ,* 67.

17. I am indebted to Hauerwas's insightful way of stating this matter: "To learn to speak Christian, to learn to speak well as a Christian, is to be habituated. Thus we are told we must speak the truth in love. The love that we believe necessary to make

Moreover, if we are what we know and love and become what we do and say, our way of speaking will be intrinsic to, and indicative of, what we are and what we hope to be by the grace of God.[18] And while most preachers will acknowledge the importance of "practicing what you preach," they give too little attention to the manner in which the character of a preacher's way of being, the conversation of one's loves, habits, and desires, is communicated as "preaching what you practice." For this reason, I suspect, Eugene Peterson laments a conspicuous absence of the practice of wisdom in ministry,

> [by which Christians] . . . uncritically embrace the ways and means practiced by the high-profile men and women who lead large corporations, congregations, nations, and causes, people who show us how to make money, win wars, manage people, sell products, manipulate emotions, and who then write books or give lectures telling us how we can do what they are doing. But these ways and means more often than not violate the ways of Jesus. North American Christians are conspicuous for going along with whatever the culture decides is charismatic, successful, influential — whatever gets things done, whatever can gather a crowd of followers — hardly noticing that these ways and means are at odds with the clearly marked way that Jesus walked and called us to follow.[19]

Arguably the most pressing need in contemporary homiletical practice is the recovery of the "preaching life" as a form of "faith seeking understanding" that renders intelligent, passionate witness to the triune God, who calls us to know him in himself and love him for himself. The Word is received through the gifts of faith and love by which the Spirit reorders human understanding and desire according to the "grammar" of Christ's self-giving in obedience to the Father. Or, as John Howard

---

our words true is not a subjective attitude, but rather, is to be formed by the habits of the community necessary for the Church to be a true witness. That is the work our speech is to do." Stanley Hauerwas, "Carving Stone or Learning to Speak Christian," in *The State of the University: Academic Knowledges and the Knowledge of God* (Oxford: Blackwell, 2007), 120.

18. Here I am following the work of Ellen Charry, *By the Renewing of Your Minds: The Pastoral Function of Christian Doctrine* (Oxford: Oxford University Press, 1997).

19. Eugene H. Peterson, *The Jesus Way: A Conversation on the Ways Jesus Is the Way* (Grand Rapids: Eerdmans, 2007), 8.

Yoder says, "The relationship between the obedience of God's people and the triumph of God's cause is not a relationship of cause and effect but of cross and resurrection."[20]

Colin Gunton and Robert Jenson have written that this logic, or what I will call "grammar," is discovered in the truth that the only begotten Word who became flesh is, himself, Jesus Christ, and that there never has been nor can there be a "Word" that is not eternally shaped to the flesh he bears. "God is certainly not otherwise the God for the creation than he is God in the gospel, and God in the gospel is who he is in the relation between the Father and that Son who — again whatever might have been — is Jesus of Nazareth."[21]

For this reason, learning the "grammar of the preaching life" is inseparable from personal knowledge of the incarnate Word that is the fruit of living, active, self-committing faith mediated through the witness of Scripture and embodied in the vulnerability of Christian witness across time.[22] John Henry Newman describes the nature of such witness in the *Grammar of Assent:*

> Instead of trusting logical science, we must trust persons, namely, those who by long acquaintance with their subject have a right to judge. And if we wish ourselves to share in their convictions and the grounds of them, we must follow their history, and learn as they have learned. We must take up their particular subject as they took it up, beginning at the beginning, give ourselves to it, depend on practice and experience more than on reasoning, and thus gain that mental insight into truth, whatever its subject matter may be, which our masters have gained before us. By following this course, we may make ourselves of their number, and then we rightly lean upon ourselves, directing ourselves by our own moral or intellectual judgment. . . .[23]

20. John Howard Yoder, *The Politics of Jesus,* 2nd ed. (Grand Rapids: Eerdmans, 1994), 237.

21. Colin Gunton and Robert W. Jenson, "The Logos Ensarkos and Reason," in *Reason and the Reasons of Faith,* ed. Paul J. Griffiths and Reinhard Hütter (New York and London: T&T Clark, 2005), 81.

22. Peter M. Candler, Jr., *Theology, Rhetoric, Manuduction: or Reading Scripture Together on the Path to God* (Grand Rapids: Eerdmans, 2006), 165.

23. John Henry Newman, *An Essay in Aid of a Grammar of Assent* (Westminster, MD: Christian Classics, 1973), 342.

Stanley Hauerwas argues that, without an adequate understanding of the kind of person they must become, more pastors will be expected to conform to uncompromising ideals. Unless pastors are formed into the particular kind of character that is capable of sustaining devotion to God and the vocation to which they are called, they will suffer from a loss of its center, or soul, and a clear sense of who they are. "I am suggesting that the character of those serving in the ministry should be determined by the character of the office to which they have been ordained. . . . In other words, there is a connection between the sacramental character of the ministry and the moral character of those who serve in the ministry."[24]

Gregory Jones helpfully describes the way Christians are located and formed in this "sacramental" identity by baptism and the Eucharist. He notes that these divinely instituted practices are central in constituting and sustaining the Christian community, forming and transforming Christian understandings of — and capacities for — making moral judgments, thus shaping and reshaping how Christians think, feel, act, and speak according to the pattern or wisdom of Christ. Baptism and the Eucharist are practices that are determinatively Trinitarian in character: baptism is done in the name of the "Father, Son, and Holy Spirit" as individuals are baptized "into Christ" by the Holy Spirit; in a similar way, the eucharistic liturgy of thanksgiving is offered for the gift of the Son's sacrifice in the power of the Holy Spirit, and after communion believers pray in the power of the Holy Spirit that they may live a life of holiness in conformity to the truth that is Christ.[25]

Given the loss of sacramental and liturgical character in our time, a pervasive temptation has been to model pastoral practice after more culturally acceptable "professions" and other forms of "communication" or "leadership." In many circles this popular strategy has contributed to the reinvention of the preacher as an "expert" who possesses the

---

24. Stanley Hauerwas, *Christian Existence Today: Essays on Church, World and Living in Between* (Durham, NC: The Labyrinth Press, 1988), 133, 135; see also Gordon W. Lathrop, *The Pastor: A Spirituality* (Minneapolis: Fortress, 2006); William H. Willimon, *Pastor: The Theology of Ordained Ministry* (Nashville: Abingdon, 2002), and *Calling and Character: Virtues of the Ordained Life* (Nashville: Abingdon, 2000).

25. L. Gregory Jones, *Transformed Judgment: Toward a Trinitarian Account of the Moral Life* (Notre Dame, IN: University of Notre Dame Press, 1990), 146-49.

right mix of techniques and skill for marketing, managing, and manipulating consumer desires through the "effective" use of knowledge and power.[26]

However, as Alasdair MacIntyre observes, "the whole concept of effectiveness is . . . inseparable from a mode of human existence in which the contrivance of means is in central part the manipulation of human beings into compliant patterns of behavior." This "moral fiction" rests on "the claim to possess systematic effectiveness in controlling certain aspects of social reality."[27]

Chris Heubner helpfully addresses this matter in regard to communicating the gospel. Because the good news of God made known in the gospel is a gift freely given, the fitting response to it will be congruent with its message, and its message — that we have peace with God in Christ — will also be its medium.[28]

What advocates of pragmatically derived pastoral "effectiveness" are inclined to overlook is the *theological reality* of ministry: "service to God by serving people who require no other service than to have their lives constantly directed to the living God."[29] Because the "preaching life" is engendered by faith in Jesus Christ, the Word made flesh who is the only begotten Son of the Father, and from whom we have received "the fullness of grace" by the outpouring of the Spirit — no amount of technical, managerial, or methodological expertise is capable of equipping a preacher for praying, thinking, and speaking in union with that Jesus. "The ministry is determined by the mission that is the church to witness to God's presence in the world through the proclamation of the Word, baptism, and eucharist, and the upbuilding of the holy."[30]

Robert Barron observes: "Christians are people dedicated to living in the truth, since Jesus described himself as the Truth (John 14:6). We who worship Jesus cannot live in falsehood, because he is the criterion

---

26. See the good summary in David E. Fitch, *The Great Giveaway: Reclaiming the Mission of the Church from Big Business, Parachurch Organizations, Psychotherapy, Consumer Capitalism, and Other Modern Maladies* (Grand Rapids: Baker, 2005).

27. Alasdair MacIntyre, *After Virtue: A Study in Moral Theory,* 2nd ed. (Notre Dame, IN: University of Notre Dame Press, 1984), 74.

28. Chris K. Huebner, *A Precarious Peace: Yoderian Explorations on Theology, Knowledge, and Identity* (Scottdale, PA: Herald Press, 2007), 131.

29. Hauerwas, *Christian Existence Today,* 140.

30. Hauerwas, *Christian Existence Today,* 136.

by which true and false are discriminated, the light in which the difference between good and evil are seen."[31] Constancy in performing the faith requires attentiveness to the grammar of the triune God revealed by the witness of Scripture, confessed in the creeds, celebrated in the church's liturgical life, and exemplified in the lives of its saints — through which we are led to know, fear, trust, love, desire, delight in, and participate in the life of the one whom we have been called to believe and sent to proclaim. Amid all the diverse situations of our lives, the Spirit creates the virtues and dispositions that enable the practice of judgment that is necessary to discern whether our preaching is making *Christian sense* — or whether we are simply talking ourselves, and our listeners, out of being Christian.

Eugene Peterson notes: "Language, one of the defining characteristics of being human, is integral to the way God reveals and works. It follows that the *way* we use language, not simply *that* we use it, is significant." When the "preaching life" is situated within — and informed by — the apostolic witness relating us to its source and goal, the God and Father of Jesus Christ, we do not need to justify our preaching by results or effects created by competitive strategies, consumer appeal, or cultural accommodation.[32]

A prayer of St. Augustine exemplifies what I will refer to as the "grammar of the preaching life." It confesses the heart's desire to know, love, and enjoy God, communicating the grammar of faith that is lived in communion with God and others.

> Grant me, even me, my dearest Lord, to know thee, and love thee, and rejoice in thee. And if I cannot do these perfectly in this life, let me at least advance to higher degrees every day, till I can come to do them in perfection. Let the knowledge of thee increase in me here, that it

31. Robert Barron, *The Strangest Way: Walking the Christian Path* (Maryknoll, NY: Orbis Books, 2004), 103.

32. Robert Louis Wilken says this: "The faith, then, is embedded in language. It is not a set of abstract beliefs or ideas, but a world of shared associations and allusions with its own beauty and sonority, inner cohesion and logic, emotional and rhetorical power. The Church's way of speaking is a collection of the words and images that have formed the thinking and actions of those who have known Christ. Christian thinking [and speaking] is inescapably historical." Wilken, "The Church's Way of Speaking," *First Things* 155 (Aug./Sept. 2005): 32.

may be full thereafter. Let the love of thee grow every day more and more here, that it may be perfect hereafter; that my joy may be great in itself and full in thee. O God, thou art a God of truth, O make good thy gracious promises to me, that my joy may be full.[33]

Following Augustine's wisdom, I assume that the preacher's first task is given in the calling of the whole church to be holy: the transformation of our humanity by receptivity to the Word and Spirit who join us to the Father through the gifts of faith, hope, and love. "Faith opens the dimension of eternity; hope makes us desire it; but love allows us to participate in it, even now."[34]

Preachers, then, will not know what they are talking about without prayerful attentiveness to the one who is God's first and final Word: "[T]he center of the activity that is Christianity cannot be an abstraction, a principle, a sensibility, or a conviction, but rather Christ himself the one from whom real assent can be elicited."[35] Moreover, the faith we confess in preaching is inseparable from the truthfulness of our words and the goodness of our lives. In addition, the capacity for hearing is the Spirit's gift that awakens the human intellect and will to the Father, whose self-knowing is a speaking, the expression of himself and all creatures in the Word out of love for his goodness. "Re-creative word does not so much break forth from the speaker as break forth in the speaker. It is rooted in a sense of the giftedness of the speaker's own being and of the giftedness of the existence in which the speaker shares communion with all being."[36] In other words, *we speak because we have first been spoken.*

In chapter 1, I attempt to clear space for a robust theological vision of the "preaching life" by providing the means to assess homiletical practice that is primarily oriented to the "effective" use of skills, methods, and techniques that tend toward abstract and pragmatic forms of faith. Chapter 1 argues for an alternative vision that is intimately re-

---

33. Cited in the worship bulletin of Christchurch Cathedral, Oxford University, Aug. 23, 2007.

34. Barron, *The Priority of Christ,* 277.

35. Barron, *The Priority of Christ,* 33.

36. David N. Power, "The Holy Spirit," in *Keeping the Faith: Essays to Mark the Centenary of Lux Mundi,* ed. Geoffrey Wainwright (Philadelphia and Allison Park, PA: Fortress/Pickwick, 1988), 167.

lated to prayerful receptivity of the Word that was communicated in creation, was spoken to Israel, became incarnate in Jesus Christ, and is mediated through Scripture and the sacramental life of the church. In other words, the truthfulness of our life and speech will reflect the first truth that has spoken us. In chapter 2, I discuss these matters with more specific reference to exemplars from the Christian tradition, St. Paul, Irenaeus, and Augustine; this serves as a transition to the second part of the book, which is a selective conversation with Thomas Aquinas and interpreters of the *Summa Theologiae,* a work that is arguably the finest example of a grammar of the "preaching life" in the Western church.[37]

Aquinas was a Dominican friar, a master of the Order of Preachers, which was founded in the early thirteenth century in response to an urgent need for evangelization and catechesis (a time that had many of the challenges that characterize our time). By means of the mission of preaching, the Dominicans played an important role during one of the most significant periods of evangelical renewal the church has ever seen. However, it is also significant that — in addition to preaching — doctrinal and biblical interpretation, the spiritual and moral life, liturgical practice, and pastoral care were also integral to this renewal. Mark Jordan describes the *Summa* of St. Thomas as a unified pedagogy of theological wisdom that served the spiritual and moral transformation of a community of preachers committed to sharing the fruits of holy teaching by following Christ, participating in and speaking of God's revealing and saving activity through him.

> The *Summa* was written to correct and rebuild certain sorts of community — to correct a community that segregated moral instruction as merely practical, to rebuild it as community in which moral in-

---

37. I have chosen Aquinas for the reasons listed in the following paragraphs of the text. My intent is not to provide a full exposition of the *Summa,* but to allow its wisdom to illuminate significant aspects of a preacher's faith, life, and work. It will be obvious that I am deeply indebted to a number of scholars whose insightful work on Thomas continues to teach me much. Although Thomas died in 1274, I believe he has much to teach us, and his "irrelevance" to our contemporary homiletical situation is an asset rather than a liability. In other words, it is precisely because Thomas Aquinas is not our contemporary that his theological wisdom is capable of challenging and addressing the circumstances of our time.

struction was central to the whole of theology. . . . The *Summa* is read whole when it is taught — taught to a community of beginners in the pursuit of integral theology. . . . The *Summa* is read whole when it is enacted as a single theological teaching, with morals at its centre and the Passion of Christ as its driving force, before a community committed to sanctification through mission, with the consolations of sacraments and liturgy, in the illuminations of contemplative prayer.[38]

In considering the wisdom of the "preaching life," we should note that Aquinas, along with other early Dominicans, united the study of Scripture and doctrine within a mystical, moral, and missional form of life in the conviction that preaching can be a way of realizing and exemplifying what it is to be holy, happy, and thus fully human in relationship to God and others, *trans*-formed to image God's holiness within the communion of Christ and his body, which is the work of the Spirit's grace. This is significant in that Thomas provides a way of understanding God's creative and redemptive action as an expression of his wisdom rather than his power and will, since "Divine Wisdom . . . is the Triune God knowing and loving himself as Father, Son, and holy Spirit, and knowing and loving all else into being as finite participations of the divine Trinitarian being."[39]

Therefore, the more we are *con*-formed to God by divine wisdom, the more we will know him, and the more we know him, the more we will be drawn to him in love, and the more we are drawn to him in love, the more we will speak and act in union with the incarnate Word, who is both our way and our goal.[40] For Thomas, the pedagogy by which God speaks the wisdom of creation and salvation — sacred doctrine — is inseparable from God's self-giving in the missions of the Word and Spirit by which the church is called, gathered, and built up, thus overcoming

---

38. Mark D. Jordan, "The Summa's Reform of Moral Teaching — and Its Failures," in *Contemplating Aquinas: Varieties of Interpretations*, ed. Fergus Kerr, O.P. (London: SCM Press, 2003), 53.

39. Matthew L. Lamb, "The Eschatology of St. Thomas Aquinas," in *Aquinas on Doctrine*, ed. Thomas Weinandy, O.F.M., Cap., Daniel Keating, and John Yocum (London and New York: T&T Clark, 2004), 226.

40. Simon Tugwell, O.P., *The Way of the Preacher* (Springfield, IL: Templegate Publishers, 1979), 31.

an understanding of theology as "content" divorced from the holiness of life that participates in God's happiness. Because God's own knowing and loving dictate the method of our knowing and loving, learning the grammar of the preaching life is dependent on divine wisdom, by which the Word and Spirit transform the full range of our human capacities: the intellect, will, affectivity, desire, bodily acts, sensate experiences, and intuition.[41] Therefore, "[f]or Christians, God's wisdom is understood primarily as Jesus, the man on the cross, a mode of address from God to us. God's wisdom is, therefore, not truth abstracted from life but truth as and in life."[42]

According to Thomas, theological and practical concerns are one for the person of prayer and virtue within the communion of friendship established by God with human creatures through the incarnation of the Word. It was thus "fitting" that God become incarnate to set us free for thinking truly *and* loving rightly, a transformation of the intellect *and* will that habituates a preacher for proclaiming *and* living the truth *and* goodness of the gospel in ways that are both intelligible *and* persuasive.

Thus are our human capacities for hearing and speaking the Word enabled, energized, and enhanced from within by divine grace rather than by external methods, rules, or obligations. Because God has revealed himself as being for the good of the other — as "other" — God's character and God's way with the world is self-giving, other-receiving love, communicated through the humanity of Jesus in union with the Word and by the power of the Spirit's grace. Hence the truth and goodness revealed in the obedience of Christ to the will of the Father in the Spirit's love confirms and enhances the co-inherence of divine influence and human freedom within the Trinitarian communion of persons. "Through the incarnation, the co-inherence of the Father and the Logos seeks to provoke a co-inherence of creation with God, and of creatures with one another."[43]

Although the work of Thomas Aquinas is widely studied by historians, theologians, philosophers, and scholars of moral theology and eth-

41. D'Costa, *Theology in the Public Square: Church, Academy and Nation,* 133.

42. Colin Gunton and Robert W. Jenson, "Christ," in Griffiths and Hütter, *Reason and the Reasons of Faith,* 16.

43. Barron, *The Priority of Christ.* Barron's argument has been most helpful for my understanding of Aquinas in this section. See also Robert Barron, *Thomas Aquinas: Spiritual Master* (New York: Crossroad, 1996).

ics, the significance of his teaching as skilled and able practitioner (as friar-preacher-theologian) deserves more attention within the field of homiletics. Yet, as Nicholas Healy has recently written about the practical ends of Aquinas's work, "[f]or Thomas the Dominican, theology is a practice which serves the apostolic church in its task of preaching the Gospel and forming its members into faithful followers of Jesus Christ."[44]

My purpose in conversing with Thomas and his interpreters will be to discern in his pedagogy a God-centered, grace-filled expression of experienced knowledge, a form of "faith seeking understanding" that is both contemplative and active, uniting prayerful attentiveness to God and a life ordered to the vocation of preaching. Thomas provides a persuasive "grammar" for the preacher's life that is derived from the heart of the apostolic message and mission: the knowledge, love, and enjoyment of God, whose goodness is revealed by the sending of the Word and Spirit, the ordering wisdom by which all things have been spoken. *We speak because we have first been spoken.*

---

44. Nicholas M. Healy, *Thomas Aquinas: Theologian of the Christian Life* (Aldershot, UK: Ashgate Publishers, 2003), 33. I have learned much from Healy's account of Thomas as a Christian theologian.

Speaking with Integrity

ROWAN Williams has written of the theological formation that is necessary if our lives are to be shaped by seeking discipline and consistency in relation to God and in forming a reflectively consistent speech for God. Williams notes that this activity, which engages all Christians and not just theologians or pastors, requires a self-awareness that asks whether our language is really talking about what it says it is talking about, or serving other purposes.[1]

Williams's concern is with Christian discourse that lacks integrity because it conceals its true agenda and thus forecloses the possibility of genuine response by stepping back from the risk of conversation, from recognizing its unfinished quality, and from the possibility of correction. He suggests that, to the degree that Christian discourse is honest, it will show in its workings what is involved in bringing the complexities of its human world to judgment before God, and will enable, without illusion, a vision of what it has set out.

> Christian reflection takes as normative a story of responses to God in the world and the world in God, the record of Israel and Jesus . . . the biblical record . . . is the kind of record it is because it weaves together history and liturgy: the God perceived in the life of Israel is constantly addressed as well as talked about. . . . The language of worship as-

---

1. Rowan Williams, *On Christian Theology* (Oxford: Blackwell, 2000). (Hereafter, page references to this source will appear in parentheses in the text.)

cribes supreme value, supreme resource or power, to something other than the worshiper, so that liturgy attempts to be a giving over of our words to God as opposed to speaking in a way that seeks to retain distance or control over what is being spoken of. . . . (p. 7)

Williams goes on to note that the overall canonical shape of Hebrew Scripture puts readers in this place of worship before God, just as the New Testament portrays the life, death, and resurrection of Jesus as the shape of God's activity in history, thus opening a direct and clear language for prayer and praise. For this reason, language about God has integrity to the extent that is directed toward God. In other words, it is in prayer, in giving ourselves to God, that who we are and what we do and say are the same (p. 7).

These comments by Williams urge us to consider the way our language about God, including the language of preaching, is kept honest to the degree that it turns on itself in the name of God, and so surrenders itself to God.

> Speaking of God is speaking to God; in prayer our language is surrendered to God in repentance, in exposure to the judgment of God, by confronting and naming its own temptations to self-deception and self-love; of its own falsehoods and self-interests: in other words, we must study the workings of our own speech, not with a sense of our own self-importance but in penitence, as a sacrifice of praise that acknowledges that we are answering to a reality, the living God, who is neither possessed nor controlled by our words, and that our speech is dependent upon the generative power of something irreducibly other than ourselves. (p. 9)

However, such awareness involves a cost: that we learn to speak truthfully by learning to see the reality of the world and ourselves in a certain way, by learning to give over what is said to the pattern of creation and redemption, a pattern that moves through loss, disorder, and death — to resurrection and newness of life. For this reason, thinking of how Christian speech can avoid becoming empty and power-obsessed is both necessary and difficult. Williams concludes that this will be required to make the discourse of faith and worship both harder, wiser, and thus more authoritative, that is, more transparent to its source (pp. 10-11). In a similar way, Thomas Long com-

ments on the need for Christians to be truthful in using words that
speak about God:

> So Christians are out there in the workaday world using words the
> best they can to increase love of God and neighbor. They speak af-
> firming words, forgiving and accepting words, words of prophetic
> challenge. But all these words are finally not enough. If we are to tell
> the truth, the whole truth, and nothing but the truth, we must ulti-
> mately speak about God. . . . [These words] are the way of God in the
> world. These are the things God is doing and saying, and we do them
> and say them because we want to shape our life according to the pat-
> tern of God's life. If we are aiming to increase the love of God and
> neighbor, then God is in the picture: God must somehow, some-
> where, be named.[2]

Williams observes that such an approach to the church's use of language goes against the grain of current practice by both traditionalists
and progressives. Traditionalists do not expect to be surprised by the
past, while progressives are not interested. Yet both miss the point:
"[W]e are all bound up in the Body of Christ, the community in which
each contributes something unique to the life of all. And this means
that the Christian will be looking and listening in his or her study of
Christian history for the way it feeds and nourishes belief now. . . ."[3]

In other words, as Chris Huebner has observed, the practices of the
whole church cultivate our Christian memory. The logic, or "grammar,"
of this memory is the wisdom of Christ's cross and resurrection. Such
memory is not simply the knowledge of past persons and events; rather,
it is a living, embodied way of life that springs from the gracious presence of Christ in the church through the witness of the Holy Spirit.[4]

Williams suggests that discerning the integrity of Christian truth
and discourse requires discerning patterns of holiness within a larger
communion in which the Spirit extends the truth and love of Christ into

---

2. Thomas G. Long, *Testimony: Talking Ourselves into Being Christian* (San Francisco: Jossey-Bass), 108.

3. Rowan Williams, *Why Study the Past? The Quest for the Historical Church*
(Grand Rapids: Eerdmans, 2005), 3.

4. Chris K. Huebner, A *Precarious Peace: Yoderian Explorations on Theology,
Knowledge, and Identity* (Scottdale, PA: Herald Press, 2007), 174.

19

the thoughts, actions, and words of faithful, salutary exemplars.[5] The church names exemplars of such truthful love, or holiness, "saints" rather than experts, remembering them not for their effectiveness or success but for lives characterized by truthful witness to the wisdom and virtue of Christ, as living sacrifices of thanksgiving to the one who alone is worthy to receive such praise.[6]

Samuel Wells describes the character of faithful performance, the church's ongoing "improvisation" of the Word that proclaims, embodies, and extends the drama of Scripture through time:

> To be a saint does not require one to have outstanding gifts or talents. All that is required is that one employ all the resources of the church's tradition . . . rather than create them for oneself, and that one long for the glory of the church's destiny . . . rather than assuming one must achieve it oneself. In the present . . . one must seek in all ways to cooperate with the other members of the company, the communion of saints, rather than stand out from them as an isolated hero.[7]

On the other hand, Craig Dykstra describes the kind of heroic, success-driven models of ministry that predominate in our time as patterns of "socially acceptable mutual self-destruction."

> [These] patterns easily survive in congregational life, no matter how much that life may be filled with a talk about sin, crucifixion, the love of God, or the grace of the Lord Jesus Christ. Indeed, the achievement-oriented congregation learns to manipulate this language well. The compulsive achiever may simply strive to be articulate about sin, convincing in an analysis of the centrality of the crucifixion in contemporary theology, effective in proclamation, purposeful and disciplined in the work of the church — all in order to earn respect and love in the congregational context.[8]

---

5. Williams, *On Christian Theology*, 27.

6. See the excellent discussion in D. Stephen Long, "God is Not Nice," in *God Is Not . . . Religious, Nice, "One of Us," An American, A Capitalist,* ed. Brent D. Laytham (Grand Rapids: Brazos, 2004).

7. Samuel Wells, *The Drama of Christian Ethics: Improvisation* (Grand Rapids: Brazos, 2004), 43-68.

8. Craig Dykstra, *Growing in the Life of Faith: Education and Christian Practices,* 2nd ed. (Louisville: Westminster John Knox), 87-88.

Arguably, the greatest challenge to contemporary Christian practice, including the practice of preaching, is loss of coherence between the church's vocation of worshiping the triune God and the character of its thought, desire, action, and speech. Dykstra observes: "The community may fall into self-idolatry. When the religious community uses its language simply for self-preservation, then God has been captured as the god of the religious cultus and is no longer the God of all of life."[9] The vocation of pastor cannot be reduced to "how to" tasks, but must be seen within a larger vision of God's sanctifying activity that engenders patterns of disciplined thinking, feeling, willing, and acting.[10]

The discourse of preaching is characterized by a particular kind of speaking that is articulated by particular kinds of speakers: women and men equipped by the gifts and empowerments of the Spirit — faith, hope, and love — that reorder human understanding and desire to God's wisdom revealed in the speech and action of Christ. Authentic speaking about God requires authentic speakers, those whose witness is characterized by congruence between the one of whom we speak and the one who speaks, wise exemplars whose lives invite us to know the one whom they know, delight in the one in whom they delight, and love the one whom they love. In short, preaching *is* theology: the homiletical expression of Christian wisdom that springs from the joy of knowing and loving the incarnate Word revealed through the whole of Scripture, whose abundant goodness is the source and end of all things.[11]

---

9. Dykstra, *Growing in the Life of Faith,* 87.

10. For example, in discussing the work of Augustine with regard to the need for truthfulness in human life and speech, Paul Griffiths notes: "Speech is the voicing of a concept. It makes thought audible by invocation as the divine word was made visible by incarnation. Duplicitous speech — the lie — divides speech from thought. It relates speech and thought inappropriately, improperly, and in doing so ruptures God's image in us. . . . Speech is a gift given, and a condition of its use is that it is received as such. But the lie is a use of speech that rejects precisely this condition by attempting, incoherently, to own speech as if it had been created from nothing by and for the speaker. This is a performative contradiction. What issues from it is an act that appears to be an act of speech but is really something else, really an absence of speech cloaked in words." Griffiths, *Lying: An Augustinian Theology of Duplicity* (Grand Rapids: Brazos, 2004), 93-94.

11. Don Saliers observes: "For Christian prayer cannot be entered into without entering into the Word of God in its fullness. To hear and to assimilate this Word in its fullness is to enter into the very life of the Word made flesh. . . . To pray is to dwell

In discussing the integrity of the church's language and life, Rowan Williams observes that what is often overlooked in assessments of its contemporary "relevance" is the question of what this language is expected to do. He suggests that the problem may not be with the language but with its users who have ceased speaking in God's presence, in relationship to the truth that is incarnate in Christ. In other words, Christian speakers easily become accustomed to using Christian language for defending, denigrating, calculating, manipulating, controlling, promoting, and any other number of lesser and idolatrous aims. Williams cites Dietrich Bonhoeffer's challenge to "religious" language, which, though he wrote it in 1944, speaks to the circumstances of our time:

> Reconciliation and redemption, regeneration and the Holy Spirit, love of our enemies, cross and resurrection, life in Christ and Christian discipleship — all these things are so difficult and remote that we hardly venture anymore to speak of them. In the traditional words and acts we suspect that there may be something quite new and revolutionary, though we cannot grasp or express it. That is our own fault. Our church, which has been fighting in these years only for its self-preservation, as though that were an end in itself, is incapable of taking the word of reconciliation and redemption to mankind and the world.[12]

Williams observes that such words are neither mistaken nor "irrelevant," as many in Bonhoeffer's time, as in ours, were quick to presume. He suggests that the challenge may be with speakers and hearers whose lives have become irrelevant to the content of Christian language, to the specific forms of faith and life within the particular community by which it is used, so that words are no longer spoken or heard as credible and trustworthy. For many, the language of faith has been reduced to a verbal tool or empty vehicle, a possession rather than a gift, and a

---

with the Word. . . . We pray with the incarnate person revealed and revealing in a Word made flesh — a mystery still veiled from our eyes, but open to our ears and the gracious affections the Spirit bestows upon the heart." Saliers, *The Soul in Paraphrase: Prayer and the Religious Affections* (New York: Seabury Press, 1980), 121.

12. Cited in Rowan Williams, *Christ on Trial: How the Gospel Unsettles Our Judgment* (Grand Rapids: Eerdmans, 2000), 37.

means that we use for achieving predetermined goals without remembering either its source or end — the great mystery of the triune God, the goodness of creation, the holiness of the church, the redemption of humanity, and the hope in the consummation of all things under the rule of the crucified and risen Christ.[13]

In *The Cost of Discipleship,* Bonhoeffer describes the form of life that will characterize the church's words and actions when shaped by God's Word in Christ through the activity of the Spirit for the recovery of true humanity.

> To be conformed to the image of Jesus Christ is not an ideal of realizing some kind of similarity with Christ which we are asked to attain. It is not we who change ourselves into the image of God. Rather, it is the very image of God, the form of Christ, which seeks to take shape within us (Gal. 4:19). It is Christ's own form which seeks to manifest itself in us. Christ does not cease working in us until he has changed us into Christ's own image. Our goal is to be shaped into the entire form of the incarnate, the crucified, and the risen One. Christ has taken on human form — became a human being like us. In his humanity and lowliness we recognize our own form. He became like human beings so that we would be like him.[14]

Because Christ unites humanity to himself in the life of his body, it is the Holy Spirit who makes the words of Scripture "relevant" — having a relationship to God and the world — through the church's embodiment of the reality of the incarnate Word in its words and its actions. "The truthfulness which we owe to God must assume a concrete form in the world. Our speech must be truthful, not in principle but concretely. A truthfulness which is not concrete is not truthful before God."[15] However, the temptation to linguistic abstraction, joined with desire for autonomy, separates the church's language from the form of life sustained by Christ's presence in history, thus creating a form of "Christianity without Christ" that stimulates more desire for religious

13. Williams, *Christ on Trial,* 38.

14. Dietrich Bonhoeffer, *The Cost of Discipleship,* trans. Reginald Fuller, rev. Irmgard Booth (New York: Macmillan, 1977), 341.

15. Bonhoeffer, *Ethics,* ed. Eberhard Bethge, trans. Neville Horton Smith (New York: Macmillan, 1965), 364.

"relevance." Bonhoeffer contends that such strategies render words incapable of truthful expression.

> It is a consequence of the wide diffusion of the public word through the newspapers and wireless that the essential character and the limits of various different words are no longer clearly felt and that, for example, the special quality of the personal word is almost entirely destroyed. Genuine words are replaced by idle chatter. Words no longer possess any weight. There is too much talk. And when the limits of the various words are obliterated, when words become rootless and homeless, then the word loses truth, and then indeed there must almost inevitably be lying. When the various orders of life no longer respect one another, words become untrue.[16]

Stanley Hauerwas comments on Bonhoeffer's assessment: "The threat to the truth for Christians comes not from the difficulty of developing an unproblematic correspondence theory of truth, but rather from the lies that speak through us disguised as truth . . . . Bonhoeffer's passion for the truth meant he would have stood against the lies that speak through us in modernity — lies all the more powerful because we believe we speak them by our own volition."[17]

Bonhoeffer perceived rightly that the temptation to make our lies true is prompted by a desire for ecclesiastical self-preservation by producing a form of popular "religion" that corresponds to the needs of the individual human psyche. Although such a privatized religion represents a withdrawal of the church from the concrete affairs of public life, it may still serve the purpose of "making individuals happy in the depths of their being" without having to ask the most decisive theological question — "of whether it is true, of whether it is the truth."

> For it could be, of course, that while religion is a beautiful thing, it is not true that it is all a nice, pious illusion — but still an illusion. But whoever so speaks [making the question of truth secondary] only sees religion from the perspective of human beings and their needs, not from that of God and his claims. . . . Only the one who has staked

16. Bonhoeffer, *Ethics,* 367.
17. Stanley Hauerwas, *Performing the Faith: Bonhoeffer and the Practice of Nonviolence* (Grand Rapids: Brazos, 2004), 67, 69. In this section I am indebted to Hauerwas's discussion of Bonhoeffer.

his or her life on Christ as the truth is in a position to judge whether Christ speaks and is the truth. . . . Truth is recognized only in the course of living it.[18]

In *Ethics,* Bonhoeffer again took up the matter of the church's conformity to the image of Christ — the unity of Christian content and form — as a requirement for seeing, living, and speaking the truth according to reality, the reconciliation of God and the world revealed in Christ. Such conformity is achieved by neither establishing programs nor applying so-called Christian principles, but in being drawn by divine grace into the form of Jesus Christ. Bonhoeffer's words speak powerfully to the conditions of our time:

> We are sick and tired of Christian programmes and of the thoughtless superficial slogan of what is called "practical" Christianity as distinct from dogmatic Christianity. . . . The primary concern is not with the forming of a world by plans and programmes. Whenever they speak of forming [the Scriptures] they are concerned only with the one form which has overcome the world, the form of Jesus Christ. . . . But here again it is not a question of applying directly to the world the teaching of Christ or what are referred to as Christian principles, so that the world might be formed in accordance with these. . . . For indeed it is not written that God became an idea, a principle, a programme, a universally valid proposition or a law, but that God became man. This means that though the form of Christ certainly is and remains one and the same, yet it is willing to take form in the real man, that is to say, in quite different guises. . . . What Christ does is precisely to give effect to reality. He affirms reality. . . . Whoever sees Jesus Christ does indeed see the world and God in one.[19]

Bonhoeffer viewed the quest for religious relevance that seeks to justify Christianity to the present age by passing the biblical message "through the sieve of human knowledge" as an evasion of reality as revealed in Christ. It is a strategy that produces a tamed, usable religion and a controlled, domesticated god — *deus ex machina* — the answer to

---

18. Bonhoeffer, *Reflections on the Bible: Human Word and Word of God,* ed. Manfred Weber, trans. Eugene F. Boring (Peabody, MA: Hendrickson, 2004), 35-36.
19. Bonhoeffer, *Ethics,* 80-81.

life's problems and solution to its needs — but a strategy that "always leads directly to paganism."[20] In *Ethics*, Bonhoeffer speaks directly to the question of whether the task of the church is to offer solutions to the world for its problems:

> It is necessary to free oneself from the way of thinking which sets out from human problems and which asks for solutions on this basis. Such thinking is unbiblical. The way of Jesus Christ, and therefore the way of Christian thinking, leads not from the world to God but from God to the world. This means the essence of the gospel does not lie in the solution of human problems, and that the solution of human problems cannot be the essential task of the church.[21]

Speaking with integrity requires that the proclamation of the gospel bring the present age before the forum of the Christian message, because Scripture is concerned with the reality proclaimed rather than immediate "relevance" according to the standards of temporal definition. True relevance, or witnessing to the truth of reality, is not where the present age announces its claims before God but where the present age stands before the truth of Christ and his claims.

Bonhoeffer saw this modern understanding of relevance as a consequence of dividing reality into sacred and secular spheres, a false separation that denied the reality of the incarnate Christ assuming the reality of the world to draw and bind it together in himself: "There are not two realities, but only one reality, and that is the reality of God, which has become manifest in Christ in the reality of the world. . . . The reality of Christ comprises the reality of the world within itself." The present is indefinable by temporal definition, but only by the Word speaking through the word of Scripture. "The relevant is and begins where God himself is his Word. The Holy Ghost is the relevant subject, not we ourselves, so the Holy Ghost is also the subject of interpretation."[22] In *Life Together*, Bonhoeffer addresses the matter of reading Scripture in light of the preacher's primary calling to serve the Word:

20. Bonhoeffer, *No Rusty Swords: Letters, Lectures, and Notes, 1928-1936*, ed. Edwin H. Robertson, trans. Edwin H. Robertson and John Bowden (New York: Harper and Row, 1965), 308-9.

21. Bonhoeffer, *Ethics*, 356.

22. Bonhoeffer, *No Rusty Swords*, 310-11.

It may be taken as a rule for the right reading of the Scriptures that the reader should never identify himself with the person who is speaking in the Bible. . . . It will make all the difference between right and wrong reading of the Scriptures if I do not identify myself with God but quite simply serve Him. Otherwise I will become rhetorical, emotional, sentimental, or coercive and imperative, that is, I will be directing the listeners' attention to myself instead of to the Word. But this is to commit the worst of sins in presenting the Scriptures.[23]

In contrast to such popular visions of religion, Bonhoeffer believed that the present is justified from beyond itself and defined by a future made known through interpretations of Scripture that bear witness to the reality of Christ, the "Lord, Judge, and Savior" who comes in the power of the Holy Spirit. The principle of such interpretation is not found in reason and experience, an intellectual or moral principle, nor a human insight or general truth that one can possess and apply as the key to understanding. If it is, the norm of presenting Scripture lies in us, and the Bible will be reduced to religious material in which this norm finds its application.[24] For Bonhoeffer, however, the whole of Scripture witnesses to Christ, the incarnate, crucified, and risen Lord who presents himself to speakers and hearers and summons the church to costly discipleship "today."

[The biblical books] set the listening fellowship in the midst of the wonderful world of revelation of the people of Israel with its prophets, judges, kings, and priests, its wars, festivals, sacrifices, and sufferings. The fellowship of believers is woven into the Christmas story, the baptism, the miracles and teaching, the suffering, dying, and rising again of Jesus Christ. It participates in the very events that occurred on this earth for the salvation of the world, and in doing so receives salvation in Jesus Christ. . . . It is not that God is the spectator and sharer of our present life, howsoever important that is; but rather that we are the reverent listeners and participants in God's action in the sacred story, the history of the Christ on earth.[25]

---

23. Bonhoeffer, *Life Together*, trans. John W. Doberstein (San Francisco: Harper and Row, 1954), 55-56.

24. Bonhoeffer, *No Rusty Swords*, 315-16.

25. Bonhoeffer, *Life Together*, 53-54.

In a startling comment, Bonhoeffer declares that the most concrete part of preaching is not the preacher's work of "practical application." It is the work of the Holy Spirit who proclaims Christ, the one who judges, commands, forgives, and calls the church through the whole witness of Scripture to faithful obedience in particular times, places, and circumstances. This Christologically and pneumatologically (Word and Spirit) centered vision confirms that wisdom is granted to those who know God through the knowledge of faith, which is given in divine revelation and necessary for seeing reality as it is.[26] In *Ethics,* Bonhoeffer says this: "The wise man is the one who sees reality as it is, and who sees the depths of things. This is why only that man is wise who sees reality in God. To understand reality is not the same as to know about outward events. It is to perceive the essential nature of things. . . . The wise man is aware of the limited receptiveness of reality for principles; for he rests upon the living and creating God."[27]

Telling the truth — or "giving effect to the truthfulness which I owe to God" — is learned in correct observation of the world and in appreciation of real situations and serious reflection on them, since the real is expressed in reference to actual concrete circumstances in consideration of who speaks, what is spoken, and to whom we speak. Learning to speak truthfully, or knowing the right word on each occasion, involves long and earnest effort, which depends on collaboration of the heart and understanding and is guided by personal knowledge of God's self-witness in Christ. "The assigned purpose of our words, in unity with the word of God, is to express the real, as it exists in God."[28]

Bonhoeffer concludes that truthfulness in preaching will require that preachers make Scripture credible rather than relevant — *in the truth that one is.*

The world's real offense is not due to ignorance, misunderstanding, or even the incomprehensibility and "irrelevance" of Christian language and concepts (i.e., Trinity, incarnation, cross, resurrection, justification, etc.), but in the church's failure to demonstrate the credibility of its language by congruence of Christian life and speech: "Because

26. Bonhoeffer, *No Rusty Swords,* 315.
27. Bonhoeffer, *Ethics,* 68-69.
28. Bonhoeffer, *Ethics,* 364, 369-70.

the church and its pastors say something different from what they do; because there is no difference between the life of a pastor and the life of a citizen. Now the way of life of the preacher is the medium of presentation. And presentation means *to make credible* so far as in us lies. Thus the question remains . . . how far we have *already made the words of the text incredible* by our life and the life of the church."[29] Interestingly, Thomas Long has voiced similar concerns about the integrity of religious speech in our time.[30]

Rowan Williams points to the way Jesus' ministry both exemplifies and enables the capacity of corrupted human beings to speak of, and enter into, communion with God and others. This is all because of the gospel we have heard and we proclaim: that in the reconciliation created by Christ in his self-abnegation, or giving away of power, we have been authorized to invite others to believe themselves to be part of a world that holds together in Christ. The reality of Christ's "kenosis," or self-emptying, which was the consensus of early Christian belief, saw in Jesus the creative newness of God, that as a whole his life and death effect the new creation. It is the Gospel narratives of Jesus — the stories of his life, death, and resurrection — that in a highly instructive sense are the speech and act of God. Paradoxically, because they create by renunciation, by giving away, we must learn to see God's creative act of love as a giving away, a letting go.[31]

Because the loving obedience of Jesus, which is the giving away of himself to God, is a response to the self-giving of God, whom he calls "Abba," God's act of speech includes a giving and receiving, a speaking and answering. "God's life is itself a movement and relation with it-

---

29. Bonhoeffer, *No Rusty Swords,* 325 (italics added).

30. "We sense . . . that amid all the God chatter and religious white noise there is a serious lack of depth, even what could be called a famine of authentic speech about God. People talk and talk and talk about God, but the language often seems empty. The God words strike the ear with the dull clink of counterfeit coins. What is missing in our culture is not God talk but authentic God talk. When the Bible, describing a particular moment in Israel's history, says, 'The word of the Lord was rare in those days' (1 Sam. 3:1), it does not mean people did not talk about God then. No doubt, people in that time spoke about God as much as ever — in houses of worship, in homes, in the marketplace. It was just that all of their God talk lacked the ring of authenticity. In short, there was a lot of God talk but very little God in it." Thomas Long, *Testimony,* 8.

31. Williams, *On Christian Theology,* 233-34.

self," as Williams puts it. Within a Trinitarian vision of reality, Jesus is the human and historical form of God's act of giving in its responsive dimension — God's answer to God, the embodiment of God's own joy in God.[32]

> To explore the continuities of Christian patterns of holiness is to explore the effect of Jesus, living, dying, and rising; and it is inevitable that the tradition of Jesus is re-read and re-worked so that it will make sense of these lived patterns as they evolve. We constantly return to imagine the life of Jesus in a way that will help us to understand how it sets up a continuous pattern of human living before God. Who Jesus is must be (and can only be) grasped in light of what Christian humanity is; but that Christian humanity is centrally characterized by the acknowledgment of dependence on a gift realized in the history of Jesus. It refuses to claim the right of self-definition or self-constitution.[33]

The work of Arthur McGill provides a helpful way of reflecting on the vision of God and humanity revealed in the person and work of Christ.[34] Following the wisdom of Scripture, McGill affirms that service, defined as the power of God, is a "shockingly impractical creed." Discussing the character of the Christian life in his book *Suffering: A Test of Theological Method,* he says:

> Self-expenditure is self-fulfillment. He who loses his life is thereby finding it. Loving is itself life, and not just a means to life. He who expends himself for his neighbor, even to death, truly lives. But he who lives for himself and avoids death truly dies: "He who does not love remains in death." (p. 57)

McGill calls attention to the need for congruence between who we are, what we believe, and how we speak, since it is the gospel incarnate in

---

32. Williams, *On Christian Theology,* 234.

33. Williams, *On Christian Theology,* 25.

34. Arthur C. McGill, *Suffering: A Test of Theological Method* (Philadelphia: Westminster, 1982). (Hereafter, page references to this source will appear in parentheses in the text.) For a more recent, excellent discussion of preaching and violence, see Charles L. Campbell, *The Word Before the Powers: An Ethic of Preaching* (Louisville: Westminster John Knox, 2002).

Christ that unites the message and messenger. If we aim to expand ourselves and our influence over others by speaking to produce effects — rather than expending ourselves in union with the Word, in the form of Christ's self-emptying — we are dead, and no matter how popular or successful our methods of speaking, our words will lack the truth and reality of God. The spirit of Jesus' ministry, serving by communicating himself to others, cannot simply be understood as a strategy chosen to produce results and effects in order to gain mastery and control over others.

> In Jesus, self-expending, therefore, was not a form he put on himself to see how well it would work. It was not a technique that he was testing to see how nicely it would help him manage his career or improve his relation with people or God. He did not stand in the carpenter's shop at Nazareth surveying his human possibilities and perhaps consulting the local library until he came to the decision to adopt service as his style. He was solely because of what God is, for he was the presence of God in the midst of men. . . . It is God's own love that stands forth in and as Jesus Christ and that informs loving self-expenditure for one another. (p. 59)

In Jesus, the Word made flesh, divine power is vindicated in that it does not dominate, manipulate, or impose itself by force or violence but serves by sharing itself. Thus the distinctive mark of God's power that works in the weakness of human beings is service, "the self-giving love which dwells with the poor and not the rich, with the sinful and not the righteous, with the weak and not the strong, with the dying and not those full of life" (p. 62).

McGill shows that, while the early church did distinguish between them, it did not divide knowledge of God's works and activity from knowledge of God's nature or inner life: *economia* and *theologia*. Following the logic of the Trinity and incarnation, McGill argues that a God who is absolute, self-enclosed and self-contained, superior and transcendent, is not the mark of divinity revealed in Jesus. He argues that to admire and bow down to God because he is immune to all need and dependence is to worship him falsely: "For the true God exists eternally — in one of his modes — as the Son — that is the state of dependence" (p. 74).

Giving careful attention to the wisdom of Scripture and the church fathers, McGill shows that, in the place of self-sufficient autonomy, pa-

31

tristic theologians saw the defining mark of divinity as the totality of self-giving and other-receiving love that proceeds between the Father and the Son: the Father gives all he has to the Son; the Son obeys the Father and offers all he has back to the Father. Thus the Father and the Son are not divine in terms of the richness of reality they possess and pass within themselves since they do not exist closed off within their own being. Rather, they are divine in terms of the richness of the reality they communicate to, and share with, the other (pp. 76-77).

Drawing from the logic, or grammar, of Trinitarian faith, McGill's work helps to illuminate our understanding of the nature of divine power and its effects on human life and speech. If force is no attribute of God, then God's divinity, as revealed in the humanity of Christ, does not consist in his ability to push things around, to impose divine will and purpose from the security of detached, self-enclosed remoteness, or to sit in grandeur while the world carries out his demands. Far from being a neutral, impersonal force, distant and external to the world, God sends his glory into the world in the form of slavery, humiliation, suffering, and death on the cross. Far from imposing, God draws near, invites, and enters into communion. Far from demanding service from others for enhancing his influence, God generously gives and expends his life in service to others for their enhancement. God acts toward the world in this way because, in himself, God is a communion of self-giving love — by exercising his powerfulness in self-giving, by how much he nourishes his creatures, and by how he fully communicates and shares his own life, reality, and goodness with them (pp. 74-77).

McGill calls attention to a significant but much overlooked theological and moral truth: "[W]e are as the power that rules us" (p. 90). Rather than asking what kind of style we should use or what methods are most effective for producing results, the preacher should more fittingly ask: "What kind of power do I worship, and what kind of power informs my life and shapes my speech?" Seen from this perspective, the conditions of human weakness that render us vulnerable before power that deprives, dispossesses, and impoverishes can easily conspire with violent and thus demonic power that kills by subordinating and subjugating those whose identity is established by their "needs."[35]

35. Robert Barron has persuasively argued that the central affirmation of classical Christianity — the incarnation of the Word — reveals the presence of a God who

Eugene Peterson suggests that the gospel is distorted when its ministry takes as its starting point human need rather than the loving pleasure of the Father, who freely and generously shares his goodness with human creatures through the Son and Spirit.

> The gospel is free, not only in the sense that we don't have to pay for it, but also in the more fundamental sense that it is an expression of God's freedom — it is not caused by our needs but by God's grace. The Trinity — not the culture, not the congregation — is the primary context for acquiring training and understanding in the pastoral vocation. . . . God is absolutely free. He doesn't do anything because he has to do it. There is no *neccesitas* in God. He is not a part of the cause-effect sequence of things. He operates out of free love — no constraints.[36]

When the tasks of ministry are understood functionally, or of necessity, for expanding one's influence by doing both to and for others, the grammar of preaching is redefined as an "effective" exercise of self-enclosed power that acts over against listeners' needs. Moreover, when this occurs, the authority of preaching will tend to be predicated on one's expertise in the use of knowledge and power rather than the joy of communicating God's incarnate knowing and loving according to the "the mind of Christ" (Phil. 2:1-11). As David Ford says, "The 'crucified mind,' shaped by the mysteries and depths of God revealed in Jesus Christ, involves wholehearted participation in the radical transformation begun in Jesus Christ. The measure of maturity is taking responsibility for one's own part in that transformation."[37]

We may understand Christ himself as God's persuasive speaking: the human form of God who evokes desire and whose power is exercised as self-giving love, which is also peace.[38] If we acquire knowledge

---

engages human creatures in a way that is neither competitive nor violent. Barron, *The Priority of Christ: Toward a Postliberal Catholicism* (Grand Rapids: Brazos, 2007), 17.

36. Eugene Peterson, "On Being Unnecessary," in Marva Dawn and Eugene Peterson, *The Unnecessary Pastor: Rediscovering the Call,* ed. Peter Santucci (Grand Rapids/Vancouver: Eerdmans/Regent, 2000), 5.

37. David F. Ford, *Christian Wisdom: Desiring God and Learning in Love* (Cambridge, UK: Cambridge University Press, 2007), 184.

38. David Bentley Hart, *The Beauty of the Infinite: The Aesthetics of Christian Truth* (Grand Rapids: Eerdmans, 2003), 3.

for extending power and producing effects rather than as a quality of speaking and living by which the Spirit communicates according to the wisdom of the Christ, its means of "effective" use will dominate rather than serve. Human weakness, deficiency, and depravity (of both the preacher and people) will be seen as flaws to be hidden and denied rather than signs of shared human dependence within a community of the Word and Spirit, the extravagant expression of God's self-giving in the crucified and risen Christ, whose strength is made complete within — rather than apart from — human weakness. Jean Daniélou comments on God's self-communication, by whom our whole being is "evangelized" by the Spirit in the form of Christ:

> The whole of the Christian life is this progressive evangelization of our being, this shedding of the flesh, selfish and closed up within ourselves, this opening up to Christ's teachings that we must follow. We must, like him, become poor; we must learn to love our sisters and brothers, and turn ourselves to the Father. . . . The Christian life consists in allowing the Holy Spirit to transform us gradually into Christ. The unique end of every person [even preachers!] is to become another Christ, because only the one who is transformed into Christ may enter into the Father's house.[39]

We are what we know and love, and we become what we do and say. Unless our lives are taken up by the Spirit for participation in the crucified "mind of Christ," which defies articulation in abstract principles and techniques, we will remain blinded by self-enclosed, self-preoccupied, self-interested desire. Because the practice of preaching requires and invites the participation of both preacher and people in the Word made flesh, it will be at home in the messiness of time, space, and history. As Robert Barron says, "Because the Word did not despise the flesh, Christians prefer to know, in Wittgenstein's phrase, 'on the rough ground.'"[40]

Ellen Charry describes the reality of such challenges to theological education because of a decrease in emphasis on wisdom and virtue in pastoral ministry: "As the American churches became more program-

39. Jean Daniélou, S.J., *Prayer: The Mission of the Church,* trans. David Louis Schindler, Jr. (Grand Rapids: Eerdmans, 1996), 73.
40. Barron, *The Priority of Christ,* 176.

matical and social service oriented, and less theologically and devotionally oriented, theological schools added more skills training to the curriculum: administrative skills, performance skills, conflict resolution skills, counseling skills, schedule and financial management skills, and social skills lead the list of things that ministers need to manage their churches and their lives."[41]

Charry observes that ministerial training and the kind of people it produces are often characterized by an approach that is similar to the process of baking a cake. Necessary ingredients in certain measured amounts must be added together in a certain order and in a specified manner. The assumption is that, if one follows the instructions contained within the recipe, the cake (i.e., one's ministry, sermons, or congregation) will turn out well. The recipe approach has replaced *education* or character formation with *training*. When schools emphasize the knowledge and skills that are required for professional success, "the student becomes like a sieve or a coffee grinder: a cipher into which material is poured in order to get a certain product on the other side." What is lost in this "production" is the transformation of the person of the student, since the purpose is no longer to educate and form excellent Christians but to train individuals who perform tasks efficiently and well (p. 4).

This kind of training creates what may be described as "theological docetism" (i.e., it only appears to be human), the loss of a theological and moral vision in which the whole of one's humanity is transformed by participating in a way of life that is constituted by knowing God, seeking the wisdom of God, and the means to attaining this wisdom, which is loving God. In short, training in skills and "how to" techniques fails to meet the most pressing need we possess as Christian people and human beings: education for knowing, loving, and enjoying the triune God (p. 5).

Charry notes that this "cookbook" or recipe approach to ministry coincides with the orientation of modern theology. She argues that the nineteenth-century "turn to the subject," which means the seeker or inquirer (that is, ourselves) rather than toward the object that is sought

41. Ellen T. Charry, "Whatever Happened to the Wisdom of God?" *Princeton Theological Review* 11, no. 2 (Fall 2006): 4. (Hereafter, page references to this essay will appear in parentheses in the text.)

(that is, God) has deeply affected the formation of pastors and their vision of God, the church, and the world. The loss of sapience, or wisdom, as the purpose of education, and the emergence of the professional training paradigm for church management and program development have changed the aim of seminary course requirements from leading students to the wisdom of knowing God to success in church growth and maintenance: "Talk of retrieving theology as knowledge seeking the wisdom of God through love reveals the great conundrum at the heart of ministerial training" (p. 6).

Nicholas Lash has challenged the dualistic assumptions of modern theology by emphasizing the integral relationship of the incarnate Word with the vulnerability of human living and speaking, since to be human is to be able to speak. Lash argues that being able to speak is to be answerable and responsible to and for each other, and to the mystery of God. In the midst of abstracted and empty God talk and idle chatter, there must be a school of silence or attentiveness, since we are constituted "as 'hearers of the word' in every fiber of our being, turned towards, and attentive to, the voice that makes us and calls us home. . . . It is, after all, Jesus who is confessed to be God's Word made flesh; it is his life, and history, and destiny, that speak to us, inviting our response."[42]

The work of philosopher Josef Pieper helps to illuminate the consequences of detaching Christian discourse from its roots, from the truth and reality of the wisdom that orders the world.[43] Because truth coheres in conversation, what we speak and how we speak must be transformed if we are to participate in the wisdom by which our lives and words are ordered truthfully. Truthful speech, then, cannot be reduced to the application of abstract, prior content in the form of principles and rules, since human creatures are made to convey, name, and identify the truth of reality with each other (pp. 16-21).

When speech is corrupted by "ignorance created by technology and nourished by information," the result is a decadence of conversation that takes the form of sophistry and flattery; the function of speech becomes more like a drug that is useful for asserting influence rather than

---

42. Nicholas Lash, *Holiness, Speech, and Silence: Reflections on the Question of God* (Aldershot, UK: Ashgate, 2004), 92, 69-90.

43. Josef Pieper, *Abuse of Language, Abuse of Power,* trans. Lothar Krauth (San Francisco: Ignatius Press, 1988). (Hereafter, page references will appear in parentheses in the text.)

saying anything of substance. Speech that has lost its connection with truth and reality is readily made an instrument of power and effectively used to manipulate others, perhaps no more so than when spoken in the name of "effectiveness" in pursuit of practical ends and results (pp. 33-34).

Pieper's insights are helpful for assessing homiletical strategies that seek to render Christianity "practically useful" by means of formulae, techniques, and programs, rather than struggling to speak the truth of God, humanity, and the world as discerned by God's wisdom. "Whoever speaks to another . . . and in doing so is explicitly not committed to the truth — whoever, in other words, is in this guided by something other than the truth, such a person, from that moment on, no longer considers the other as partner, as equal. In fact, he no longer respects the other as a human person . . ." (p. 21). In the end, notions of "communication" that lack the coherence of Christian wisdom effectively diminish the dignity of the speaker, what is spoken, and those who listen.

> It is entirely possible that the true and authentic reality is being drowned out by the countless superficial information bits, noisily and breathlessly presented in propaganda fashion. Consequently, one may be entirely knowledgeable about a thousand details and nevertheless, because of ignorance regarding the core of the matter, remain without basic insight. . . . The place of authentic reality is taken over by an infectious reality; my perception is indeed still directed toward an object [in the case of preaching, God], but it is a pseudo-reality, deceptively appearing as being real, so much so that it becomes almost impossible any more to discern the truth. (pp. 33-34)

Speech that is ordered wisely will be true, though not because it proves "effective" in producing results, creating effects, and expanding influence, or that it is superbly crafted, brilliantly formulated, or strikingly delivered. Rather, it is because it seeks to communicate the truth of reality with as little distortion and omission as possible (pp. 18-19).

Paul Griffiths' exposition of Augustine's treatise *On Lying* brings clarity to the moral consequences of human speech that turns from God to the self.[44]

---

44. Griffiths, *Lying,* 94. (Hereafter, page references will appear in parentheses in the text). Griffiths concludes by saying that "it is an element of central importance in

Sin's characteristic work is displayed in self-serving aversion: sinners turning their faces away from God and attempting, narcissistically, to look only at themselves. Sin's result is damage, as sinners exchange a free gift of infinite value for a circumscribed piece of low-rent real estate whose freehold they hope to own by their own unaided efforts. The exchange defeats itself: even as sinners make the gesture of aversion and the grab for ownership, they know they have made a strange bargain. (p. 55)

Lying occurs when we live for ourselves and our own ends, following the desire to live autonomously, which takes our nature, experience, and needs as the truest guide for thinking and speaking. We consequently end up living and speaking for ourselves, turning inward on ourselves rather than turning toward God as the true end of life and happiness (p. 86).

Griffiths shows that, for Augustine, lying is a desire to own the gift of speech that in reality belongs to God. This is due to neither misunderstanding nor ignorance but rather expropriation, the theft of language, a distorted act of the will that claims to be good for us but really is bad for us. Thus the deep desire for happiness or beatitude, the fruit of loving the truth that is God, becomes duplicitous when joined with forms of life that represent its contradiction. We cannot find the cure for this disease in ourselves; we can only discover it by turning to God, by looking to God and returning to God's Word in adoration, by participating in God as the "beautifully radiant source of truth and goodness" (pp. 87-88).

Augustine's analysis of what it is like to be a speaker: a user of language, under the sign of sin. The lie is the ideal type of sinful speech, speech distorted by disordered desire. . . . Augustine's analysis of what's wrong with the lie is carried on always as a counterpoint to his recommendation of confession and adoration as the only kind of non-sinful speech. . . .

"It is, instead, an attempt to depict what it would be like to turn the gaze away from the lie toward the truth — which is to say, toward God . . . an offer always to be understood as an act of the Triune God, the God who created the cosmos, who elected a people, who became incarnate, who was crucified and resurrected, who orders and inspires the church, and who makes himself available for our contemplation and consumption in the Eucharistic worship of the same church. The lie is speech under the condition of sin: speech transformed by God's gift is the praise-shout of the church" (pp. 225-26).

Rowan Williams suggests that this particular form of speaking wisely will have the status of exile and refugee in the world. It will also sound strange to a church tempted to secure its own survival or success in the religious marketplace by its use of "effective" means at the expense of human vulnerability and need. This will be especially true for those who are called to preach, since it is false and even arrogant to believe that we are responsible for managing and controlling the results, effects, or outcomes of proclaiming the Word. Williams captures this well:

> We speak because we are called, invited, and authorized to speak, we speak what we have been given, out of our new belonging, and this is a dependent kind of utterance, a responsive speech. . . . The integrity of theological utterance, then, does not lie in its correspondence to given structures of thought, its falling into line with an authoritative communication, but in the reality of its rootedness, its belonging, in the new world constituted in the revelatory process. . . . God "speaks" in the response as in the primary utterance: there is a dimension of "givenness," generative power, and the discovered world in the work of the imagination opening itself.[45]

If the aim of the preaching life is participation in the reality of God's saving action, it will submit itself to be worked out in the history of weak and sinful people revealed in and through the contingencies of Israel's and Jesus' history. As Lash notes, "In the Fourth Gospel the truth which shall make us free is truth enfleshed, enacted, made finite and particular, arrested, tried, and crucified; but it is not truth sought elsewhere." The truth we are authorized to speak and live by is received in the appropriation of vulnerability, the form of God's self-giving; the incarnate knowing and loving by which the world is renewed.[46]

The integrity of preaching is defined by the church's primary vocation, the joy of praising and knowing God, to which we have been called in our baptism. It is a lifelong education through union with Christ in his passion and resurrection, following and imitating the Word through whom we return ourselves and our words to the one whose self-

---

45. Williams, *On Christian Theology,* 146-47.

46. Lash, *The Beginning and the End of 'Religion'* (Cambridge, UK: Cambridge University Press), 247-48.

giving is the originating source of all that is. Through the Spirit's grace we are schooled in the life of holiness to become glad recipients of — and truthful respondents to — God's re-creative Word. *We speak because we have first been spoken.*

The Preaching Life
as Exemplary Wisdom

[handwritten: But Don't preach what the people hear. / Popular. · lead the people to worship True God]

ACCORDING TO the witness of Scripture, the perennial challenge confronting the church in its vocation of worshiping the true God truly is not cultural irrelevance, as is widely believed in our time. Rather, it is idolatry, the worship of false gods and those more subtle forms of idolatry that, in the name of being "Christian," absorb and subordinate the true God as a means to lesser ends. Indeed, our most "deeply felt need" will always be fidelity to the God of Jesus Christ, who lovingly creates, calls, and redeems us for a life that is a sacrifice of thankful praise. The great Shema of Deuteromony summons Israel to offer exclusive worship and devotion to God through every aspect of living as God's covenant people in the world.

> Hear, O Israel: The Lord our God, the Lord is one. Love the Lord your God with all your heart and with all your soul and with all your strength. These commandments that I give you today are to be upon your hearts. Impress them on your children. Talk about them when you sit at home and when you walk down the road, when you lie down and when you get up. Tie them as symbols on your hands and bind them on the door frames of your houses and on your gates. (Deut. 6:4-9)

And while preaching the Sermon on the Mount, Jesus confirmed the vocation of Israel for his disciples, revealing himself as its source, substance, and scope.

> Do not think that I have come to abolish the Law or the Prophets; I have not come to abolish the Law or the Prophets; I have not come to abolish but to fulfill them. I tell you the truth, until heaven and earth disappear, not the smallest letter, not the least stroke of a pen will by any means disappear from the Law until everything is accomplished. Anyone who breaks one of the least of these commandments and teaches others to do the same will be called the least in the kingdom of heaven, but whoever practices and teaches these commands will be called great in the kingdom of heaven. For I tell you that unless your righteousness surpasses that of the Pharisees and the teachers of the law, you will certainly not enter the kingdom of heaven. (Matt. 5:17-20)

These words may be a surprise to many contemporary preachers, since the conventional wisdom of our time presumes that conformity to cultural expectations *(sola cultura),* of either conservative or liberal inclination, and at either the elite or popular level, offers the best hope of salvation for the church. However, such shortsightedness tends to overlook the reality of preaching as a gift of the Spirit that transforms the church to hear, believe, and embody God's saving wisdom revealed and enacted by Christ. Nicholas Lash comments on the challenge of idolatry:

> All human beings have their hearts set somewhere, hold something sacred, worship at some shrine. We are spontaneously idolatrous — where, by "idolatry", I mean the worship of some creature, the setting of the heart on some particular thing (usually oneself). For most of us there is no single creature that is the object of our faith. . . . Idolatry is the divinizing, the taking of absolute and over-riding of any value, fact, nation, dream, project, person, possession or idea. It matters not what being I take as god and set my heart upon, whether it be freedom or efficiency, yesterday or tomorrow, America or me; to make of some being, of any being, an "absolute", an object of worship, is idolatry.[1]

---

1. Nicholas Lash, *The Beginning and End of 'Religion'* (Cambridge, UK: Cambridge University Press, 1996), 21,134, 245; I have been assisted by the interpretation of Christendom and modernity in Douglas Harink, *Paul Among the Postliberals: Pauline Theology Beyond Christendom and Morality* (Grand Rapids: Brazos, 2003). See esp. the conclusion, "Preaching Paul: Beyond Christendom and Modernity."

When seen from this perspective, pragmatically derived methods that characterize much contemporary ministry are simply incongruent with the constitutive wisdom of Christian preaching: the overflow of loving delight and thankful praise to the triune God, the fitting response to a generosity and foolish abundance far beyond all needs and practicality. Tom Long has described a kind of functional talk that presumes to speak about God but actually talks about other things in place of God.

> Sometimes church folk talk about God, but it is just a form of pious marketing. We say "worshiping God gives life new meaning" when we are really trying to grow church membership. We say "prayer changes things," but we are really attempting to entice someone to join our prayer group, to reinforce our own religious patterns, and to reassure ourselves that our beliefs are right. . . . Authentic religious language is not about some narrow band of experience called "religion" in "church" or our little view of God's will. . . . Whenever we take the words that describe this fullness and melt them down into something smaller, more manageable, and self-centered, we have gone to the mountaintop but come away with a golden calf. It is idolatry.[2]

Because the character of the triune God is self-sharing love and desire, overflowing excess, abundance, generosity, and delight, God's work of salvation — the fullness of human life in God's presence — implies an invitation to participate in the joy of loving God and others in God. The Father sends the Word and Spirit *(missio dei)* to create habits enabling an acknowledgment of divine truth and goodness as the source and power of our being and the end of all human yearning, need, and desire. Thus it is the gospel of Jesus Christ that engenders the true ethic *(ethos)* from which all worship, preaching, evangelism, and mission spring and to which they return as an offering of joyful praise in communion with God.[3]

It is this deep sense of joy, the fruit of being known, desired, and loved by God through the sending of the Word and Spirit that sustains preachers for the vocation of proclaiming a gospel that communicates

---

2. Thomas G. Long, *Testimony: Talking Ourselves into Being Christian* (San Francisco: Jossey-Bass, 2004), 24.

3. Here I am indebted to David F. Ford and Daniel W. Hardy, *Living in Praise: Worshiping and Knowing God,* rev. ed. (Grand Rapids: Baker, 2005).

— and is communicated by — the wisdom and power of a crucified Lord. Daniel Hardy and David Ford argue persuasively that we have no reason to preach the gospel other than sheer love, enjoyment, and appreciation of and for God. They say that the most "useful" or "relevant" form of Christian communication is praise-centered rather than problem-centered.

> Recognizing and responding to God inevitably leads to evangelism and mission as acts of love and celebration, longing for others to share in something whose delight increases by being shared. Yet expressions of praise easily become overbearing and triumphalistic, as does evangelism. When this happens, there is a contradiction of the message. The history of evangelism is extremely painful, full of examples of the message being falsified by the way it is spread. The crucifixion of Jesus is the only essential guard against this. It contradicts all glib praise and preaching. It continually demands the repentance, re-conversion, suffering and even death of the evangelist. This is not just a matter of method, as the temptations of Jesus show the classic traps of evangelism — the use of worldly incentives, spectacular events and manipulative power. The alternative is the way of the cross, from which the true ethic [ethos or character] of evangelism springs: an ethic of radical respect which refuses any coercive communication, preferring to suffer and die, but which also refuses to compromise on what is communicated.[4]

It is significant that the apostle Paul, in addition to the deep affection and anguish that he felt for his communities, regularly appealed to the dramatic transformation he had undergone to demonstrate his embrace of the wisdom embodied by the Lord whom he followed and proclaimed: the weakness of crucifixion and power of resurrection. Thus, not only did Paul's message, but also his life as messenger, communicate the wisdom of the gospel, so that life emerging out of death must be manifest in him. Ellen Charry observes:

> The first Christian theologian prepared Christians for the world's inability to comprehend their vision of human dignity and happiness. I Corinthians 1:18-31 begins: "For the message of the cross is foolish-

---

4. Ford and Hardy, *Living in Praise,* 190.

ness to those who are perishing, but to us who are being saved it is the power of God. . . ." Paul's message remains a stumbling block to Jews and foolishness to pagans. But those who know themselves bound up in the life of God are free from the power of the world, for they flourish by knowing and loving God.[5]

Arguably the most important means of persuasion for Paul's preaching was his ethos, which was a visible way of instructing communities and answering critics.[6] For example, in 2 Corinthians 3, Paul describes himself as a captive to the one whom he proclaims: by his participation in the wisdom of the cross he was drawn daily into a way of suffering and death to become a *living sacrifice* of praise to the God of Jesus Christ. This is indeed a startling confession and self-characterization, a form of "reverse ethos" by which Paul seeks to distinguish himself from other preachers who were, by his accounting, "hucksters" who "peddled" God's word in antiquity's marketplace of religion.[7]

> But thanks be to God, who always leads us in triumphal procession in Christ and through us spreads everywhere the fragrance of the knowledge of him. For we are to God the aroma of Christ among those who are being saved and those who are perishing. To the one we are the smell of death; to the other, the fragrance of life. And who is equal to such a task? Unlike so many, we do not peddle the word of God for profit. On the contrary, in Christ we speak before God with sincerity, like men sent from God. (2 Cor. 2:14-17)

Paul defends his apostolic ministry by arguing that the integrity of his preaching was the affect of — and affected by — the power and wisdom of the cross, just as the aim of his pastoral work was to form a people whose primary love and loyalty would be directed to the crucified Lord, who took the form of a servant, humbling himself to death on a cross in loving obedience to God.

5. Ellen T. Charry, *By the Renewing of Your Minds: The Pastoral Function of Christian Doctrine* (New York: Oxford University Press, 1997), 3.

6. See the excellent discussion of Paul in Andre Resner, Jr., *Preacher and Cross: Person and Message in Theology and Rhetoric* (Grand Rapids: Eerdmans, 1999); see also David S. Cunningham, *Faithful Persuasion: In Aid of a Rhetoric of Christian Theology* (Notre Dame, IN: University of Notre Dame Press, 1991).

7. See Resner, *Preacher and Cross,* for a full discussion of "reverse ethos."

We need to preach the wisdom of cross. No new method and style.

WE SPEAK BECAUSE WE HAVE FIRST BEEN SPOKEN

It is on account of this gospel that the particular qualities embodied by Paul, in both his speech and life, provided a stark contrast to the popular, culturally attuned characters in Corinth, who prized the effective use of words for extending their influence over others. More was at stake for Paul than differences of homiletical method and style. It was the God-given means and end of pastoral work: the transformation of the church by the Spirit into the image of God's incarnate Son. Therefore, Paul's practical wisdom, which was oriented toward the end to which the church had been called through the preaching of the cross (i.e., the story of the crucified Christ), illuminated the way by which the church was to embody that wisdom in the presence of God and the world.[8]

And while Paul acknowledged that his ministry was marked by hardship, rejection, and suffering, it also provided a visible means of contrasting himself with opponents whose speech was marked by rhetorical eloquence and power. Andrew Purvis notes: "People who come so preaching will be slick communicators, homiletical masters — Paul calls them 'super apostles.' They will know how to work the crowds with their facile speech. Undoubtedly, they will be a great success in the pulpits of power. But in the knowledge of God and the Gospel they will fall short of the mark."[9]

Paul makes the startling claim that authority to speak and be heard is found in the visible relationship between the mode of speaking, the character of the speaker, and the wisdom of what is spoken. Guarding against temptations to use preaching as a means for status or self-promotion by asserting his intellectual, emotional, or rhetorical skills, Paul's manner of speaking was one of weakness and deliberately lacking in eloquence — so that God's power would be manifested from faith to faith. The comments of David Ford and Frances Young portray the nature of the "preaching life" as practiced by Paul:

8. Here I am following James W. Thompson, *Pastoral Ministry According to Paul: A Biblical Vision* (Grand Rapids: Baker, 2006), and *Preaching Like Paul: Homiletic Wisdom for Today* (Louisville: Westminster John Knox, 2001). See also the extensive discussion in Michael J. Gorman, *Cruciformity: Paul's Narrative Spirituality of the Cross* (Grand Rapids: Eerdmans, 2001).

9. Andrew Purvis, *Pastoral Theology in the Classical Tradition* (Louisville: Westminster John Knox, 2001), 124.

In the service of the Gospel, Paul claims, there can be both an ultimate urgency with accompanying authority, and also a self-effacement eliminating any pride in oneself except insofar as one is corresponded to one's message. To be identified with this message is to be in union with one who was poor, humble, weak, and dead. If this is how true power comes from God, then it must involve a critique of other sorts of power, authority and effectiveness, and of all boasting and pride.[10]

Integral to the proclamation of the gospel will be congruence between the preacher and preaching. Proclaiming the gospel witnesses to the reconciliation of a preacher to the "foolish wisdom" of Christ, just as the credibility of the gospel is enhanced by the conformity of the church to his "weak power." Thus, for Paul, "Christ himself has become the power of God and the wisdom of God in deliberate contrast to secular definitions of wisdom. . . . And this same Christ, the wisdom of God, is himself the message of 'God-breathed' Scripture: in the context of faith in Christ, they 'are able to make you wise unto salvation'" (2 Tim. 3:15).[11] Mark McIntosh expresses it this way:

> This vision is what most crucially marks the Spirit filled mind of Christ. It is a vision utterly free from fearful grasping, and in its confidence in the Father's love it is the outpouring (Spirit) of that divine generosity within the constraints of the broken world. . . . For the church is simply those bits of the whole creation called up into a new pattern of relationship in which, however faintly and fitfully, something of the divine pattern of relationship can be recognized and sought. . . . And this means that the particular pattern of communal thinking identified as the mind of Christ is the pattern of knowing and loving in which all creatures are called to share. . . . This freely self-giving love of Christ becomes, by the power of the Holy Spirit, the very structure of a new kind of talking and thinking and being with one another.[12]

10. Frances Young and David F. Ford, *Meaning and Truth in 2 Corinthians* (Grand Rapids: Eerdmans, 1987), 210.

11. Markus Bockmuehl, *Seeing the Word: Refocusing New Testament Study* (Grand Rapids: Baker, 2006), 81.

12. Mark McIntosh, "Faith, Reason, and the Mind of Christ," in *Reason and the Reasons of Faith,* ed. Paul J. Griffiths and Reinhard Hütter (New York/London: T&T Clark, 2005), 135.

If the message of the cross is true to reality, that God has chosen to save the world through the "foolish wisdom" of a crucified savior, a message whose efficacy does not depend on either human ingenuity or skill, then proclaiming the gospel will be an intrinsically liberating and joyful affair. Preaching will be an act of praise that summons listeners to become glad recipients of the generous outpouring of self-giving love by the crucified and risen Lord, the one who speaks and acts in the fullness of the Spirit's power. In our time, as in Paul's, the life and speech of preachers — the "preaching life" — which is shaped by the power and wisdom of Christ crucified, will be integral to faithful gospel proclamation. Ellen Charry sums it up well:

> Now the point of 1 Cor. 1:18-31 is that those who grasp the wisdom of the cross are truly wise. They seek nobility, status, power, and dignity in their proper place: the cross. From this vantage point they see that the standards of the world are vacuous and that one's proper dignity is to be found in knowing oneself to be a child of God by the power of the cross of Christ. If Jesus' death is the means of making one a child of God, all proper power and authority derive from this relationship and no other source. Worldly power is irrelevant to who we really are. . . . Excellence comes from learning what God has done on a grand public scale that sets one's life in a fresh context and gives it new direction and meaning.[13]

The work of Rowan Greer demonstrates that the early church maintained a steady conversation between theology and ecclesial life. Those who were charged with elaborating technical theology were also preachers in the church whose aim was to articulate and shape the experience of ordinary Christians. For this reason, doctrine and life were one. The church's worship was not simply an appropriation of the past, but was a present, corporate experience of God articulated by the church's faith. The preacher's task was to put into words the wisdom of what the church was being given to apprehend and know: its present appropriation of the Savior and his saving work in the world.[14]

13. Charry, *By the Renewing of Your Minds*, 42-43.
14. Rowan A. Greer, *Broken Lights and Mended Lives: Theology and Common Life in the Early Church* (University Park, PA: Pennsylvania State University Press, 1986), 1-20.

Greer's discussion of the intimate connection of theology and life in the early church helps bring into focus the modern separation of theology and practice, or content and form, because, according to patristic wisdom, Christian lives are the best apology for the truth of the gospel. In our time these divisions have contributed to a separation of theological convictions and the life of the church, so that much pastoral and church practice remains untested by Christian wisdom, and much Christian wisdom is uninformed by pastoral and ecclesiastical practice. However, faithful preaching of the gospel requires a reconciliation of theology and practice grounded in, and demonstrated by, truthful witness to Christ, which is manifested by the concrete reality of the church: "The Christian vision is meant to be translated into virtue: the faith that apprehends God's gratuitous forgiveness in Christ must be translated into radical obedience to him."[15]

For this reason, the grammar of the preaching life is learned through participation in a form of life that is enlivened by the Spirit to participate in, and witness to, the restoration and renewal of humanity, on the way from Pentecost to the return of Christ, which is itself an expression of the gospel. On the other hand, when the gospel is abstracted from the apostolic witness that joins us to Christ, it is easily accommodated to criteria external to his life, speech, and the gospel.[16]

The Christian tradition has overwhelmingly affirmed that a preacher is called to become a particular kind of person who participates in a particular vocation for the formation of a particular people who exist to worship a particular God; a particular way of thinking, loving, and speaking thus suffuses the humanity of the preacher with the wisdom and holiness of Christ. This is essential if the church is to hear — through the medium of Scripture and the vulnerability of human witness — the voice of the risen Lord, who transforms its life according to

---

15. Greer, *Broken Lights and Mended Lives*, 12.

16. Eric O. Springsted says of Paul: "Faith then comes through the hearing of the good news, the preaching of the resurrection (Rom. 10:14-15). Believing the gospel is a personal response of obedience (Rom. 10:16). The form of that faith is love (Gal. 5:6), which is exercised within a community formed by that preaching and animated and unified by Christ himself. Indeed, faith which is exercised within this community and makes sense within it can thus be said to be created by the preaching itself." Springsted, *The Act of Faith: Christian Faith and the Moral Self* (Grand Rapids: Eerdmans, 2002), 87.

creation's final end: the fullness of love for God for God's sake, and love for neighbors in God.

Irenaeus, the second-century bishop of Lyons in southern Gaul, wrote extensively to defend the incarnation of the Word who mediates the anointing of the Spirit, arguing that the salvation of humanity begins with the humanity of Jesus and is inseparable from union with the incarnate Lord, who is its source and end. Irenaeus turned repeatedly to the baptism of Jesus to show the continuity between Old Testament promises and New Testament fulfillment. The anointing of Christ in the Jordan has cosmic significance, since the Father anointed and adorned all things through him, while the Father also has the initiative for the incarnation, by which the Word assumed our humanity to effect its restoration and renewal through the anointing of the Spirit.[17]

According to Irenaeus, God eternally anoints the Word with the divine Spirit, precisely as God; but through the incarnate Word, God also anoints the whole of the created universe with the Spirit. Kilian McDonnell comments:

> In the waters of the Jordan, he receives his salvation history anointing, a claim which Jesus makes in reference to his baptism. "The Spirit of the Lord is upon me." At this moment, Jesus is anointed Savior because he is the cause of salvation to those who are freed from all kinds of ills and from death. He is savior also to those believers who come after them, on whom he confers salvation. . . . Again at the Jordan, the Father anointed this man with the Spirit, in virtue of which he takes on his saving mission, to preach good news to the poor, to free from all manner of ills and from death, and to give eternal salvation to others who believe in him.[18]

McDonnell emphasizes that this double anointing, the Word in the heart of the Father, and the Lord in time at the Jordan, has messianic significance related to this mission. According to the prophetic tradition, the Expected One was to receive the Spirit's anointing and imparting of the seven gifts (Isa. 11:2-4), empowering him to carry out his sav-

---

17. I am following the excellent discussion in Kilian McDonnell, O.S.B., *The Baptism of Jesus in the Jordan: The Trinitarian and Cosmic Order of Salvation* (Collegeville, MN: Liturgical Press, 1996).

18. McDonnell, *Baptism of Jesus,* 58-59.

ing mission. Because the Lord was conceived by the Spirit, at his baptism receiving the Spirit in order to communicate it to others within the economy of salvation, the gift of the Spirit is now clothed with the humanity of Christ. For Irenaeus, the theology of the church begins with the movement of the triune God toward humanity through the Word and Spirit, engendering a way of knowing that is received through the church's worship and sacramental life, its prayer and catechesis, and the words, images, and narratives of Scripture in its preaching.[19]

According to Irenaeus, the vocation of humanity consists in beholding the glory of God revealed in the incarnate Word. Moreover, this calling is inseparable from the concrete, visible life of the church, since "God respects our time and body boundedness" by working within them. "God graciously gives himself, the entire Trinity, to dwell in the human being . . . engaging the human being's own characteristic powers of knowing and loving without ceasing to be their entire activity."[20]

The sending of the Son and Spirit reconciles human creatures to participate in the divine life, knowing and enjoying the salvation willed by the Father for the whole created universe. Moreover, the Spirit who anointed Jesus at the Jordan was poured out at Pentecost, thus reconciling the nations to be a visible manifestation of God's saving activity in the world. Commenting on Irenaeus's view of the incarnate Christ as the perfection of the *imago Dei,* A. N. Williams writes of a "fleshly" doctrine of the body "that is not destitute of participation in the constitutive wisdom and power of God."

> Participation in God means knowing God and enjoying his goodness. The chief enabler of sight is not this light — which seems unlikely to be material — but the literal flesh-and-blood manifestation of the Word, who made the divine nature, which is beyond comprehension and boundless and invisible, visible and comprehensible to believers. . . . "The glory of God is a living human person and human life consists in beholding God."[21]

---

19. McDonnell, *Baptism of Jesus,* 59-60, 237-47.

20. Eugene F. Rogers, "Faith and Reason Follow Glory," in *The Theology of Thomas Aquinas,* ed. Rik Van Nieuwenhove and Joseph Wawrykow (Notre Dame, IN: University of Notre Dame Press, 2005), 453.

21. A. N. Williams, *The Divine Sense: The Intellect in Patristic Theology* (Cambridge, UK: Cambridge University Press, 2007), 34.

McDonnell similarly emphasizes the significance of the baptism for communicating to humanity the eternal anointing of the Son by the Father, demonstrating the coherence of first creation (Genesis) with second creation (redemption) in the unity of the Son's divinity and humanity (Jesus and Christ) through the Spirit's anointing. Moreover, because the anointing at the Jordan is set in the revelation of the Trinity and the mysteries of Christ, the Spirit now rests on all humanity. It is the Spirit's anointing of Jesus that is a sign of the cosmic salvation accomplished by the sending of the Son, the imparting of the Spirit, and the giving of the messianic gifts of wisdom, understanding, counsel, strength, knowledge, godliness, and piety, or fear of the Lord. "The Spirit rests on Jesus and in Jesus. Later, the risen Christ dispenses the Spirit to believers out of his own fullness. And all believers are baptized in a single Spirit. In the Son and by the power of the Spirit, believers become sons and daughters of God, sharers in the divine life."[22]

According to Irenaeus, the salvation of humanity begins with the Word incarnate in Jesus. The Son imparts the Spirit by which the Father anointed him to unite us with himself, making us participants in the mission of God, which is "recapitulated,"or summed up, in the events of Jesus' life, death, resurrection, and ascension. McDonnell says:

> The Spirit descends on Jesus so that the Spirit might get accustomed to dwell in the human race. The Spirit rests on us as the Spirit descended and rested on Jesus, anointing him at his baptism. This anointing is an expression of the fullness of the gifts of the Spirit imparted to Jesus, a sign of what the gifts of the Spirit mean in the Christian life. . . . The Father anoints others, the prophets, the just, the disciples, with the Spirit, giving also access to the Father through the Word and only through the Word. . . . The vocational holiness of the Church is in and by the Spirit dispensed by the Risen Christ in baptism, and is in the Son and by the power of the Spirit, a created participation in the inner-Trinitarian movement as it enters history in the plan of salvation through the missions of the Son and the Spirit.[23]

It is no coincidence that in *Teaching Christianity,* arguably the most influential handbook for preachers in the history of the Western

---

22. McDonnell, *Baptism of Jesus,* 118-20.
23. McDonnell, *Baptism of Jesus,* 122-23, 237.

We are body of the church and part of Christ.

church, St. Augustine affirmed the essential unity of theology and spirituality, prayer and preaching, Christian language and life. Just as Christ the incarnate Son is fully human and fully divine, and as the crucified, resurrected, and exalted Lord rules at the Father's right hand, so Christ, as head of the church, indwells and evokes the prayer and praise of his body through the Spirit's self-giving love.[24] For Augustine, then, the church is called to become the public embodiment of the saving wisdom and holiness revealed in the incarnate Word, replicated by the words of Scripture and proclaimed through the words of its preachers.

Augustine thus wrote as a teacher of preachers to communicate a participating way of knowing that unites thought and life and unfolds in devotion to God through the apprehension of Christian wisdom. This conversion proceeds through seven stages by which a person is drawn from bondage to beatitude, a movement of ascent toward God that is carried by love and imparts spiritual habits, or dispositions, for understanding and communicating the truth of Scripture. By following this particular way, we humans reorient our desire to Christ, the one whose wisdom and humility — truth taking on human nature — purifies the mind and heart through knowing and loving God in a life of holiness.[25]

This is primarily a matter of believing God with one's heart, soul, mind, and strength, a pilgrimage leading to "the Father, the Son, and the Holy Spirit, a single Trinity." This pilgrimage is constituted by the

24. This essay includes revised sections from my book *Christian Preaching: A Trinitarian Theology of Proclamation* (Grand Rapids: Baker, 2006). For Augustine, the primary text I am using is *The Works of Saint Augustine: A Translation for the 21st Century, De Doctrina Christiana [Teaching Christianity]*, 1:11, ed. John E. Rotelle, O.S.A. (Hyde Park, NY: New City Press, 1996). (Hereafter, references to this source will appear as DDC in parentheses in the text.) For a good introduction to Augustine's pastoral theology, see Mark Ellingsen, *The Richness of Augustine: His Contextual and Pastoral Theology* (Louisville: Westminster John Knox, 2005).

25. For my reading of Augustine, I am indebted to the interpretation of A. N. Williams, *The Divine Sense*, 143-89, and Williams, "Contemplation," in *Knowing the Triune God: The Work of the Spirit in the Practices of the Church*, ed. James J. Buckley and David S. Yeago (Grand Rapids: Eerdmans, 2001), 121-46. See also J. Patout Burns, "Delighting the Spirit: Augustine's Practice of Figurative Interpretation," in *De Doctrina Christiana: A Classic of Western Culture*, ed. Duane W. H. Arnold and Pamela Bright (Notre Dame, IN: University of Notre Dame Press, 1995), 182-94. On Augustine's theological reading of Scripture as leading to union with God in holy love, see Michael Dauphinais and Matthew Levering, *Holy People, Holy Land: A Theological Introduction to the Bible* (Grand Rapids: Brazos, 2005).

virtues of faith, hope, and love through the work of sanctifying grace, which reorders one's thoughts and affections to participate in the double commandment of love. Augustine concludes: "So, if it seems to you that you have understood the divine scriptures or any part of them, in such a way that by this understanding you do not build up this twin love of God and neighbor, then you have not understood them" (DDC, I.36.40).

Love of God and holiness of life compose the content and form of the preaching life. Augustine invites his readers to a hermeneutic fitting for its subject: the wisdom of humility that cleanses the mind from worldly distractions and reorders desire by the movement of the Spirit's love. As Russell Reno observes of Augustine's work, "We are dynamic creatures who are defined by our loves. We move toward that which we love. In Augustine's view, we quite simply are the weight of momentum of our loves. . . . We are made for love, and our desire is to give ourselves away, not to draw in upon ourselves as the source and ground of our happiness."[26]

Knowing God as the triune and incarnate mystery is central to attaining this end, since it is not a matter of words, or of ideas or concepts, but is essentially knowing the truth of reality: the heart of the Christian mystery is the fact of God made man, God with us in Christ, which is a matter of believing and adhering to God's saving wisdom revealed in him. To become a preacher requires not only believing something, learning something, or even knowing how to do something; but it is to become a certain kind of person by belonging to a community, by being a participant in the spiritual and moral discipline that incorporates us into the mystical body of Christ and the church.[27]

Book II of *Teaching Christianity* discusses the study of Scripture as the way to holiness of life, an ascent to God with the mind and heart through the practice of prayer and the Spirit's gifts (DDC, II.7.9-12). Beginning with the fear of the Lord, Augustine inverts the order of Isaiah 11 to culminate with the enjoyment of divine wisdom that constitutes peace with God's will. While fear raises the thought of death and judgment, it also checks pride and self-love, thus making room for the gift of

---

26. R. R. Reno, "Pride and Idolatry," *Interpretation* 60, no. 2 (April 2006): 170-80.

27. Andrew Louth, *Discerning the Mystery: An Essay on the Nature of Theology* (Oxford: Clarendon Press, 1983), 73-74.

humility. The second gift is purity, which opens us to the truth of Scripture and grants confidence in its trustworthiness in our hearing, speaking, and living.

Fear and piety, humility and receptivity give way to the knowledge of God that is acquired through the study of Scripture. And while this includes the study of languages and other forms of knowing, its scope is the whole of Scripture, since it is in discerning the fullness of scriptural wisdom that we "know" the incarnate Word who is the way and goal to God. This way of reading directs attention from the self to God, increasing one's self-knowledge, an awareness of one's enmeshment in sin, while strengthening one's love for God and the neighbor. For Augustine, knowing Scripture enkindles hope that everything in creation and in history is the work of divine wisdom, communicated by the reality of the Word and apprehended through the gift of faith in the form of love.

As the basis of prayer, hope strengthens courage for us to continue hungering and thirsting after righteousness and desiring God's goodness. Moreover, courage prevents despair, turning us away from loving things to loving God, evoking the joy of participating in the communion of Trinitarian love. The fifth step is the counsel of mercy, the cleansing of troubled souls by the power of forgiveness that enkindles love for the neighbor and will include even one's enemies. The sixth step leads to deeper cleansing of one's vision, through which wisdom becomes clearer, more pleasant, and enjoyable to increase one's love for the truth — rather than the self, others, and things — beside which there is no greater reward.

> In this manner, the love of truth comes to characterize a person so that she cannot be turned aside by concern to please another person or to seek her own advantage, even and especially when interpreting Scripture. Purified and prepared, she finally ascends through knowledge to wisdom, knowledge of God that is communion with him, and that for which we have been created, the vision of God.[28]

The union of prayerful study and spiritual purification engenders a transformation that unfolds according to the pattern of God's incarnate wisdom, the "Word made flesh." This conversion is attained by lov-

---

28. Burns, "Delighting the Spirit," 187.

ing God with the intellect and will, a way of humble love and adoration by which we return the gift of words to the one who knows and speaks all things through the self-emptying of Christ. For Augustine, as Paul Griffiths notes,

> [t]rue speech is disowned, relinquished, returned as gift to its giver, definitively and universally not yours. . . . To speak truly is to accept the gift of speech by adoration. . . . To speak the word of adoration is to speak Christ: just as God incarnate returns God's gift by way of the self-abnegation on the cross, so thought invoked returns God's gift by way of the self-abnegation that is adoration. . . . Adoration removes speech's necessity by being taken up into participation; crucifixion removes its necessity by being taken up into resurrection.[29]

Augustine directs attention to the subject of Scripture: the God who is contemplated and adored in the church's worship, doctrine, and life. The end of all human knowing and loving is the Father, Son, and Holy Spirit, the holy Trinity, the one being who is the living God. Moreover, the triune God is known through the gift of wisdom that enkindles desire and directs the intellect to find its rest and enjoyment in loving communion with himself. Here Augustine's vision differs significantly from pragmatic and utilitarian approaches to God, others, and the world that are familiar in our time.

> Some things are to be enjoyed, others to be used, and there are others, which are to be enjoyed and used. Those things, which are to be enjoyed, make us blessed. Those things, which are to be used help, and, as it were, sustain us as we move toward blessedness in order that we may gain and cling to those things, which make us blessed. If we who enjoy and use things, being placed in the midst of things of both kinds, wish to enjoy those things which should be used, our course will be impeded and sometimes deflected, so we are retarded in obtaining those things which are to be enjoyed, or even prevented altogether, shackled by an inferior love. (DDC, I.3.3)

The formation of preachers occurs in contemplation, or prayerful attentiveness, loving God with the intellect and will, through a way of

---

29. Paul J. Griffiths, *Lying: An Augustinian Theology of Duplicity* (Grand Rapids: Brazos Press, 2004), 85, 91.

knowing engendered by discerning the truth of Scripture and participating in the pattern of its life. This cultivates a sense of theology —
theologia — that is best defined as a habit of thinking, loving, and acting
— *habitus* — a disposition that has the character of personal knowledge
of God and the things of God, and has the character of wisdom —
sapientia — in relationship to the mystery of God. Thus the gift of God's
illuminating operation of the intellect is directly tied to prayer, the virtues, and passionate desire and affection for God.[30]

Learning to speak wisely is integrally related to learning to pray,
think, love, and live within a community that exists to praise, know, and
enjoy the one who speaks himself and his goodness through the creation and redemption of all things. Seen from this perspective, problems related to reading and preaching may often be more a matter of
foolish pride, ingratitude, darkened vision, unreasonableness, false
loves, bad habits, and disordered desires than deficiencies in herme-
neutical theory or homiletical method and technique. As the practice of
wisdom, or the knowledge we live by, preaching is learned best through
participation in "the school of Christianity, whose pedagogy has the
two-fold purpose of weaning us from our idolatry and purifying our desire."[31] Because the language of preaching is inseparable from the language of worship, our thinking and speaking are most truthful when ordered by a "grammar" that leads to union with Christ in love for God, as
God, and loving for neighbors in God.[32]

Augustine directs his readers' attention to the Word, who is
known with the intellect and loved with the will, thus joining prayer
with the study of Scripture, the activity of preaching, and the gift of
the Spirit, whose loving makes us holy. "Lacking concepts in the mind
and words on the tongue we cannot speak what we do not know, but if
we do not love the God to whom the words lead, we do not under-

---

30. Edward Farley, *Theologia: The Fragmentation and Unity of Theological Education* (Philadelphia: Westminster Press, 1983), 34-35.

31. Lash, *The Beginning and the End of 'Religion,'* 21.

32. Eric Springsted observes: "Thus faith for Augustine is a personal transformation by the Word through the words heard and spoken. To have faith is not just to
think something, as thinking with assent; it is to think actively by listening to and
learning from the Word, which is ever personal both in intent and in delivery. It is to
take that Word to heart and live by it. That is what it is to participate in God, to be
taken up into God's own life." Springsted, *The Act of Faith,* 147.

stand."[33] Loving contemplation of the incarnate Word transforms one's way of being, living, and speaking into a sacrifice of thankful praise to God. A. N. Williams describes this vision:

> To be a Christian meant assenting to certain propositions as true, as well as undergoing baptism in the triune name, and the church was adamant in rejecting syncretism; to accept baptism and profess the creed during the initiation rite meant disassociating oneself from other religions and philosophies. These hallmarks of identity reflect a Christian anthropology and soteriology, inasmuch as they presume the involvement of the whole human person in the initiation rite; the mind, grasping the content of the creed; the will, assenting to it; and union with Christ in body and soul in the sacrament of washing. . . . The baptismal liturgy . . . integrally linked intellectual understanding, assent and worship, which is precisely what contemplation is.[34]

Augustine concludes that a preacher must become "an eloquent sermon" and *"a person who prays"* (DDC, IV.33). Through the working of divine grace *and* human receptivity, it is possible for the interpreter of Scripture to become a living interpretation of Scripture: "The life that is an 'eloquent sermon' is always a work in progress. It is an exploration of the meaning of love for God and neighbor, of following the humble way of Christ . . . the daily life of someone trying to embody Scripture within the highly specific circumstances of community life . . . learning the meaning of love for God and neighbor by practicing it."[35] Within the liturgical devotion of the church, newly given memory, understanding, and will are received according to the law of prayer and believing — *lex orandi, lex credendi* — two distinct but intimately related expressions of one grace that engenders the wisdom of Christian identity and action, *lex operandi:* "faith originating in God and communicated . . . through human means which [are] themselves suffused with faith."[36]

It would be difficult to overestimate the importance of prayer for

---

33. Robert Louis Wilken, *The Spirit of Early Christian Thought: Seeking the Face of God* (New Haven: Yale University Press, 2003), 311.

34. Williams, *The Divine Sense,* 14.

35. Rebecca Harden Weaver, "Guidance for the Pilgrim Community," *Interpretation* 58, no.1 (Jan. 2004): 41.

36. Aidan Kavanaugh, O.S.B., *On Liturgical Theology* (New York: Pueblo Publishing, 1984), 98-99.

Augustine's understanding of Christian speech because, for him, the measure of theology, which begins when we first pray, lies in its power to enkindle knowledge and love of its subject, which leads to happiness. Therefore, if human happiness is the joy of knowing God within the Trinitarian communion of love, the language of preaching will find its truest expression as doxology, orthodoxy — or *right praise*. Augustine gives this elegant description in a homily for the day of Pentecost:

> And then the Spirit, pervading him thus with the fullness of richer grace, kindled his hitherto frigid heart to such a witness-bearing for Christ, and unlocked those lips that in their previous tremor had suppressed the truth, that, when all on whom the Holy Spirit had descended were speaking in tongues of all nations to the crowds of Jews collected around, he alone broke forth before the others in the promptitude of his testimony on behalf of Christ. . . . And if anyone would enjoy the pleasure of gazing on a sight so charming in its holiness, let him read the Acts of the Apostles (2:5) and there let him be filled with amazement at the preaching of the blessed Peter, over whose denial of this Master he had just been mourning; there let him behold that tongue, itself translated from diffidence to confidence, from bondage to liberty, converting to the confession of Christ the tongues of so many of His enemies, not one of which he could bear when lapsing himself into denial. And what shall I say more? In him there shone forth such an effulgence of grace, and such a fullness of the Holy Spirit, and such a weight of most precious truth poured from the lips of the preacher, that he transformed that vast multitude. . . .[37]

Such happy apprehension and loving adoration of God spring from a preacher's life in eloquent expressions of spiritual truth and wisdom. Through experienced habits of reading and speaking — the fruit of knowing the truth and loving the good — the living Word leads a pilgrim people toward *alteras civitas* ("another city") and the transformation of all things in God. For Augustine, then, theological speech in this life is inevitably bound up with the vision of God in the next.

---

37. Cited in Elizabeth A. Dryer, "Spirituality as a Resource for Theology: The Holy Spirit in Augustine," in *Minding the Spirit: The Study of Christian Spirituality,* ed. Elizabeth A. Dryer and Mark S. Burrows (Baltimore: Johns Hopkins University Press, 2005), 188.

That is why, since we are meant to enjoy the truth, which is unchangeably alive, and since it is in its light that God the Trinity, author and maker of the universe, provides for all the things he has made, our minds have to be purified to enable them to perceive that light, and to cling to it once perceived. We should think of this purification process as being a kind of walk, a kind of voyage to our home country. We do not draw near after all, by movement in place to the One who is present everywhere, but by honest commitment and good behavior. (DDC, I.10.10)

For Augustine, the character or ethos of the preacher is the most important factor in the activity of preaching. Becoming a preacher is to have the quality of one's language and life transformed to become a truthful witness to Jesus Christ, God's incarnate wisdom who creates what we are, gives substance to what we know and love, informs what we speak and do, and reorders our lives to what we shall be by God's grace (DDC, IV.27.59).[38]

This "grammar" is learned within a way of life that unites prayer and preaching, contemplation and action, in a manner analogous to the incarnation. The whole life and ministry of Jesus is the work of God in which the Son of God, anointed by the Spirit, takes to himself our fallen world — our sinful, human flesh — and lives in it a life of faithful, loving praise on our behalf, doing the will of the Father, walking according to God's wisdom, speaking and following God's way. In his vocation Jesus learned for us the wisdom we have lost through sin and foolishness; he has overcome our idolatrous, unjust, and destructive ways, and has restored and brought to completion our lives as creatures made to share the image of God. Fully God, he descended into ignorance and humiliation; fully human, he advanced in wisdom and character to demonstrate his full participation in our creaturely life, "for us and for our salvation" in loving communion with God.[39]

---

38. Of the spiritual and moral import of knowing God, A. N. Williams observes: "To think of God has consequences for how one prays and to think of God is the beginning of prayer; all theology must therefore be taken as spiritual theology, just as all prayer rests on dogmatic assumptions and bears dogmatic implications and is in some measure a form of theological reflection." Williams, *The Divine Sense*, 236.

39. Colin E. Gunton, *Theology Through Preaching* (Edinburgh: T&T Clark, 2001), 79-84.

Augustine invites preachers to know, love, and enjoy the God who redeems us for sharing his life through faith, hope, and love (DDC, I.12-14.13). By immersing themselves in the truth of Scripture, and by listening to and learning from God, pastors acquire the gift of wisdom, which engenders the authority of faith that thinks with assent and is moved by God's gracious activity. Robert Wilken observes:

> Augustine wishes to say that the knowledge acquired by faith is not primarily a matter of gaining information. The acquiring of religious knowledge is akin to learning a skill. It involves practices, attitudes, dispositions and has to do with ordering one's loves. This kind of knowledge, the knowledge one lives by, is gained gradually over time. Just as one does not learn to play the piano in a day, so one does not learn to love God in an exuberant moment of delight. If joy does not find words, if it does not exercise the affections and stir the will, if it is not confirmed by actions, it will be fleeting as the last light out of the black west. The knowledge of God sinks into the mind and heart slowly and hence requires apprenticeship. That is why, says Augustine, we must become "servants of wise men. . . ." Authority in Augustine's view does not impose or coerce, it enlightens. Its appeal is to the understanding, not to the will. A good teacher does not strong-arm students or make appeals to status or position . . . but earns confidence by experience, knowledge, insight, and, finally, truth.[40]

For the contemplative life, Christ is the wisdom *(sapientia)* that makes foolish all the so-called wisdom of human systems of thought; but for the active life, he is the practical wisdom *(prudentia)* that finds its most profound expression, not in any system of speculative thought or rhetorical eloquence, but in the humble wisdom of the cross — *sermo humilis* (humble speech).[41] Thus *sapientia* and *prudentia,* end and means, are united in Christ. For Augustine, homiletical excellence is the fruit of personally knowing, loving, and delighting in the "Word made flesh," which is its source, way, and goal.

---

40. Wilken, *The Spirit of Early Christian Thought,* 172, 175.

41. Jaroslav Pelikan, *Divine Rhetoric: The Sermon on the Mount as Message and as Model in Augustine, Chrysostom and Luther* (Crestwood, NY: St. Vladimir's Seminary Press, 2000), 101.

> Therefore Christ is our knowledge, and at the same time Christ is also our wisdom. He himself plants faith in us concerning temporal things; he himself shows forth the truth concerning eternal things. Through him we reach on to him: we stretch through knowledge to wisdom; yet we do not withdraw from one and the same Christ.[42]

Commenting on these words, Michael Hanby says: "[I]n the person of Christ God binds Creator and creature, time and eternity, heaven and earth, God and humanity into the most intimate of unions, simultaneously disclosing the eternal union of triune love in the temporal love of Christ, and drawing us, through Christ, into that same love."[43]

Without the gift of wisdom, engendered by faith and love that direct the intellect and will to God's self-communication in Christ, fidelity to the Word is easily sacrificed for the sake of ends less than God.[44] Only the presence of the indwelling Word and Spirit are able to create the joy of communion with God whose incarnate wisdom binds the knower and the known, the lover and the beloved.[45]

The Christian wisdom of Paul, Irenaeus, and Augustine bears little resemblance to the timeless, atemporal language, or "words about words," that is produced by the modern lure of technical reason. As Nicholas Lash observes of our human capacities for making sense of

---

42. Cited in Michael Hanby, *Augustine and Modernity* (New York: Routledge, 2003), 57.

43. Hanby, *Augustine and Modernity,* 56.

44. Williams, *The Divine Sense,* 165-66.

45. Here the comments of Russell Reno are relevant: "Augustine's own theory of human action and his view of the person predict such an outcome [rebellion against God]. Self-love is unstable, because it seeks to live for the sake of the self, and we cannot rest in ourselves as the alpha and omega of our own lives, 'You stir man to take pleasure in praising you,' he famously writes in the first paragraph of his *Confessions,* 'because you have made us for yourself, and our heart is restless until it rests in you.' (I.I). Because of this deep fact about human beings, since we can never succeed in turning inward upon ourselves in self-love, we can no more stop seeking to praise God than we can stop breathing. For this reason, we need to convince ourselves that the sinful structure of our lives is actually an appropriate strategy for praising and serving the highest good. Our heart tells us that only God can give us rest, so we wrap our love of worldly things in the false tinsel of divinity and propose them to ourselves as idols worthy of worship. This strategy of self-deception allows us to pursue the finite goods of creaturely life as if they were images of the divine life." Reno, "Pride and Idolatry," 180.

things, speaking truth, and acting with integrity: "But all these things we do from somewhere, shaped by some set of memories and expectations, bearing some sense of duty borne by gifts that have been given. All sense, and truth and goodness, are carried and constituted by some story, some pattern of experience, some tradition."[46]

The authority of preaching is derived from the one who is its source, way, and goal: God's Word incarnate in Jesus Christ. Ephraim Radner puts it this way: "Authority has to do with a common set of beliefs and a common way of life . . . and that there are people who have a particular set of virtues that allow them both to understand these beliefs and ways better than others to protect and augment them in the midst of life's chances and changes."[47] Rather than more "effective communicators," we need preachers who possess the virtue of practical wisdom that will enable them to discern and speak faithful improvisations of life in the Spirit with the "mind of Christ" according to the grammar of self-giving love.[48] This will require that theory and practice, knowing and doing, are united by wisdom, the gift and capacity that enables us to "see" clearly in particular times, places, and circumstances.[49]

Thomas Aquinas, the thirteenth-century master preacher and teacher of preachers as a member of the Dominicans (the Order of Preachers), serves as an exemplary witness to Christian wisdom, which entails "love of God, union with God, revelation, and a union of the theoretical and practical. The task of theology [and preaching as one of its expressions] is thus one part of the exercise of wisdom in love."[50] Thomas's best-known work, the *Summa Theologiae*, unites contemplating the triune God with preaching and living the gospel in faithful obedience to Christ, "the way that has been stretched out to us into God."

46. Lash, *The Beginning and End of 'Religion,'* 21.

47. Ephraim Radner, "The Scriptural Community: Authority in Anglicanism," in *The Fate of Communion: The Agony of Anglicanism and the Future of a Global Church*, ed. Ephraim Radner and Philip Turner (Grand Rapids: Eerdmans, 2006), 105.

48. See the discussion of "improvisation" in David F. Ford, *Christian Wisdom: Desiring God and Learning in Love* (Cambridge, UK: Cambridge University Press, 2007), 192ff.

49. Thus does David Ford describe the contemporary quest for wisdom, for discerning meaning, truth, and right conduct in life and speech. Ford, *Christian Wisdom*, 2.

50. Ford, *Christian Wisdom*, 268.

Instead of better speaker, the preacher needs wisdom. Speak with the mind of Christ.

Thomas Aquinas and the Dominicans:
Ordering the "Preaching Life"

T HE ORDER of Friars Preachers, or the Dominicans, was born during a thirteenth-century upsurge of evangelical fervor and mission activity that pressed for the renewal of the Roman Catholic Church from both inside and outside official ecclesiastical sanctions and structures. In 1206, the founder of the order, Dominic of Guzman (1170-1221), was deeply involved in preaching Christian doctrine against particular forms of dualism, the heretical teaching of the Albigensians and Cathars, while en route through southern France with Diego, his bishop from Osma, in Spain.[1]

The heterodox Gnostic groups Dominic was opposing were positing a universal conflict between good and evil, the material and the spiritual, and were winning converts through their popular preaching, pastoral care, and ascetic way of life. This posed a number of challenges to official Roman Catholic doctrine and practice, and it created an urgent need for a well-informed and devoted clergy, which was made all the more pressing by the emergence of an increasingly articulate and critical laity. Dominic's spiritually and intellectually rigorous response to these heretical groups, his "holy preaching," was the inspiration for the founding of the Dominicans as an order that was dedicated to em-

---

1. C. H. Lawrence, *Medieval Monasticism* (New York: Longman, 1984), 193-210. For a description of twelfth- and thirteenth-century heresies, see Malcolm Lambert, *Medieval Heresy: Popular Movements from the Gregorian Reform to the Reformation* (Oxford: Blackwell, 1992), 35-146.

bodying the apostolic mission of the gospel within a movement of itinerant, mendicant preachers.[2] Pierre Mandonnet notes:

> The founding of the Order of Friars Preachers was very closely bound up with the general needs that were making themselves felt in the Christian world at the start of the thirteenth century. Having encouraged religious life in this new stage of development, the church of Rome decided to make use of it in order to solve some of the urgent problems confronting the church. . . . The ministry needed an ecclesial militia that was both well-educated and directly in contact with the social life of the times. The Friars preachers with their new kind of religious life and original mode of organization were the answer to the needs of the new age.[3]

The Dominicans were a movement of traveling preachers who vowed to imitate what they pictured as the simple way of humility, obedience, and poverty — the evangelical life characterizing the preaching ministry of Jesus according to Luke 10. They presented a compelling alternative to the stability of noble families, rich merchants, careerist clergy, and settled monasteries.[4] In 1215, the bishop of Toulouse (in southern France) issued a document in support of the newly formed band of preachers, "instituting Dominic and his companions as preachers . . . to root out heresy, drive out vices, teach the rule of faith, and imbue people with right morals."[5] In 1216, the order was approved as an Order of Preachers but was neither confined to any diocese nor dependent on any bishop for its mandate to preach: "[O]ur Order is

---

2. Allan White, O.P., "The Foundation of the Order of Preachers and Its Historical Setting," in *The Way of the Preacher,* by Simon Tugwell, O.P. (London: Darton, Longman & Todd, 1979), 97-110; see also Nicholas M. Healy, *Thomas Aquinas: Theologian of the Christian Life* (Burlington, VT: Ashgate, 2003), 24-33; 1-14; "Introduction," in *Early Dominicans: Selected Writings,* ed. Simon Tugwell, O.P. (Mahwah, NJ: Paulist Press, 1982), 1-48; R. W. Southern, *Western Society and the Church in the Middle Ages* (London: Penguin Books, 1970; reprint 1990), 279-84.

3. Cited in Thomas O'Meara, O.P., *Thomas Aquinas: Theologian* (Notre Dame, IN: University of Notre Dame Press, 1997), 6.

4. Tugwell, "Introduction," in *Early Dominicans,* 12.

5. Cited in John Van Engen, "Dominic and the Brothers: *Vitae* as Life-forming *exempla* in the Order of Preachers," in *Christ Among the Medieval Dominicans,* ed. Kent Emery, Jr., and Joseph P. Wawrykow (Notre Dame, IN: University of Notre Dame Press, 1998), 9.

known to have been founded initially precisely for the sake of preaching and the salvation of souls, and all our concern should be primarily and passionately directed to this all important goal, that we should be useful to the souls of our neighbors."[6]

The Dominicans were not simply people who were available for the task of preaching as might be needed, but they were by right and definition a particular kind of order whose members earned their living by preaching and pastoral care, pursuing a life of prayer and study to become living instruments of the Word. "Here was a guild of preachers . . . [whose] purpose was to preach, to craft words. . . . Preached words provided the tools for a learning and eloquence that would act as a purging fire for all those who had fallen into error, but for all the indifferent faithful, the instruments of a warm, enkindling fire."[7]

Sharing in the agitations and miseries of growing cities and urban dwellers, the preaching friars sought to embody the apostolic and missionary dimensions of the gospel as both their message and way of life. Joining serious study and the way of Christ with a commitment to poverty, humility, and dependence on the grace of the Holy Spirit, they were a mission of evangelization and catechesis that aimed to bridge the gap between learned preachers and uneducated listeners. Uniting the ministry of the Word to hearing confessions, the order was shaped by theological and moral wisdom that was embodied by a community of preachers who were guided by the gift of holy teaching and moved by the virtue of charity to mediate the truth of Christianity to all walks of life. What stands out most of all about this order that was sent out by Dominic on a mission that would extend throughout and beyond the boundaries of Christendom was its zeal for the salvation of souls, as directed by the the order's *Primitive Constitutions*:

> They shall set forth and shall everywhere comport themselves as men who seek to obtain their own salvation and that of their neighbor, in all perfection and the spirit of religion; like evangelical men following in the footsteps of their Saviour, speaking with God and of God, either with themselves or with their neighbors. . . . When they thus set forth to exercise the ministry of preaching, or to travel for any other reason,

6. "Early Dominican Constitutions, " quoted in Tugwell, *Early Dominicans*, 457.
7. Van Engen, "Dominic and the Brothers," 22.

they are not to receive or carry any gold, silver, or coin or any other gift except food, clothing, and other necessary equipment, and books.[8]

The Dominicans, then, were an order identified by preaching as their central activity: the fruit of prayerful and diligent study emerging from and leading to the contemplation of God and all things in relationship to God, a union rooted in faith and love through which all practical ends are rightly discerned and achieved. To this end, the Dominican Order required that the wisdom of the preaching life be informed and inspired by the gift of divine charity that would bear much fruit through a generous outpouring of human speech in union with the Word active in creation, redemption, and incarnate in Jesus Christ.[9]

For the Dominicans, the most crucial factor to be observed in a preacher is the "grace of preaching," since what makes preaching different from a lecture, speech, or cultural entertainment is the grace of the Spirit that enters and affects the minds and hearts of its participants by way of their hearing the gospel. Despite the Dominicans' huge success, they recognized that, in addition to hard work, training, and talent, ultimately the Holy Spirit is the one who teaches the art of preaching, granting not only human eloquence but a "divinely attractive word."[10] Only God is able to call, equip, and send preachers to speak a living word to a dying world, "just as God will at the end of time, raise up dead bodies by his word, so he now gives life to dead spirits by the power of his word."[11]

Education for the Preaching Life

Both Dominican education and practice was committed to doctrinal preaching — communicating the saving truth of Christian faith — which was an activity reserved for the clergy and which required constant immersion in liturgical, intellectual, and moral training. Commenting on the work of Thomas Aquinas, David Burrell describes the

8. Tugwell, *Early Dominicans,* 467.

9. Tugwell, *The Way of the Preacher,* 82-96.

10. Tugwell, *Early Dominicans,* 181-82; see also the excellent discussion on the grace of preaching in Tugwell, *The Way of the Preacher,* 33-41.

11. Humbert of Romans, "Treatise on the Formation of Preachers," in Tugwell, *Early Dominicans,* 201.

integration of Dominican forms of worship with learning to think and speak the truth of the Christian faith:

> Something more is required: something akin to the practices of a faith community . . . [which] at once presuppose as well as prepare us to acknowledge a "metaphysics of participation" according to which the universe in which we quite naturally live becomes de-centered in such a way to become a created world. In this way, "spiritual exercises" become part of metaphysics . . . language use and metaphysics interpenetrate . . . and the intentional link between them will be reflected in a "form of life" embodying a characteristic set of practices. . . .[12]

The Dominicans learned to contemplate the truths of the faith in their liturgy, in their fourfold reading of Scripture, and in catechesis centered on the Articles of Faith: "There is abundant evidence that Dominicans understood the liturgy as a continuous meditation on, and recreation of, the acts revealed in the Articles of Faith (the Creed), that they read the Bible, not as a secular history book, but as a multifaceted revelation of Christ; and that their devotions, and even daily routines of conventual life were designed to steep the brothers in the life of Christ."[13]

Thus an integrative theology uniting the regeneration of the intellect, the purification of desire, and the cultivation of moral discernment for living and speaking the gospel characterized preachers who were equipped to respond in pastorally appropriate ways to new challenges and threats. The Dominicans' evangelical message was inseparable from the order's preachers, whose lives were sustained by the joy of communicating the truth of God's revealing and saving activity in Christ. The order thus embodied a particular form of life aspiring to display the reality of the gospel in the lives of humble preachers who vowed to follow Christ by imitating the example of his followers described in the apostolic witness of Scripture.[14]

The early *Dominican Constitutions* exemplify the order's approach

---

12. David Burrell, C.S.C., "Analogy, Creation, and Theological Language," in *The Theology of Thomas Aquinas,* ed. Rik Van Nieuwenhove and Joseph P. Wawrykow (Notre Dame, IN: University of Notre Dame Press, 2005), 94.

13. Joseph Goering, "Christ in Dominican Catechesis: The Articles of Faith," in Emery and Wawrykow, *Christ Among the Medieval Dominicans,* 135.

14. Healy, *Thomas Aquinas,* 24-27.

to careful examination of its preachers to determine what grace of preaching they possessed and to inquire about their habits of study, religious life, eagerness of charity, and commitment and intention to the vocation of preaching. Preachers who displayed sufficient evidence in these areas were sent out, while others were assigned to further study and practice under the supervision of more experienced brothers.[15] And while study was not an end for members of the order, it was a necessary means for securing its end: contemplation of the truth of God that overflows into teaching and preaching for the salvation of souls, since without study neither could be accomplished.[16] Because of the ends the Dominicans served, theological inquiry and preaching as means to that end were a matter of life and death.[17]

Thomas Aquinas

Best known among the Dominican masters is Thomas Aquinas (d. 1274).[18] His life and work as a member of the Order of Preachers demonstrates that intellectual love of God, undertaken with full seriousness and embracing the whole of life, can itself be a genuine form of piety, provided it is motivated by charity and a desire for knowing and communicating the truth of God's wisdom with others. This vocation immersed Aquinas in a God-centered way of life that included not only the intellect but also intentions, dispositions, actions, and words. In thirteenth-century terms, Thomas's task was threefold: *legere, disputare, predicare*

15. Tugwell, *Early Dominicans,* 466-67.

16. Southern, *The Middle Ages,* 298-99.

17. Simon Tugwell, "The Spirituality of the Dominicans," in *Christian Spirituality: High Middle Ages and Reformation,* ed. Jill Raitt in collaboration with Bernard McGinn and John Meyendorff (New York: Crossroad, 2001), 15-25.

18. See the excellent introduction in *Albert and Thomas: Selected Writings,* trans. and ed. Simon Tugwell, O.P. (Mahwah, NJ: Paulist Press, 1988), 201-352. See also the discussions of Aquinas in Jean-Pierre Torrell, O.P., *Saint Thomas Aquinas,* 2 vols., trans. Robert Royal (Washington, DC: Catholic University Press, 1996-2003); Healy, *Thomas Aquinas: Theologian of the Christian Life;* O'Meara, *Thomas Aquinas: Theologian;* Aidan Nichols, O.P., *Discovering Aquinas: An Introduction to His Life, Work and Influence* (Grand Rapids: Eerdmans, 2002); Fergus Kerr, O.P., *After Aquinas: Versions of Thomism* (London: Blackwell, 2002); M.-D. Chenu, O.P., *Aquinas and His Role in Theology* (Collegeville, MN: Liturgical Press, 2002).

— to comment on Scripture, to debate doctrinal questions, and to preach before both academic and popular audiences. Hence, study and prayer share the same goal and belong to the same charitable movement of *imitatio Christi*, a movement that, as ecclesiastical and liturgical, overflows into the active life of teaching and preaching.[19]

Thomas's work was to discuss the teachings of Scripture and the truths of the faith by means of the church's reflections on those teachings in a pedagogically appropriate way. His task was to display the consistency of those teachings, to refute misunderstandings and erroneous interpretations, and to deepen an understanding of and desire for the gospel so that it might be preached more convincingly and lived more obediently.[20] A prayer of Aquinas that Dominican brothers recited before dictating, writing, or preaching — *Ante Studium* ("before study") — captures the spirit and shape of this work:

> Ineffable Creator,
>
> Who, from the treasures of Your wisdom, have established three hierarchies of angels, have arrayed them in marvelous order about the fiery heavens, and have marshaled the regions of the universe with such artful skill,
>
> You are proclaimed the true font of light and wisdom, and the primal origin raised high beyond all things.
>
> Pour forth a ray of Your brightness in the darkened places of my mind; disperse from my soul the twofold darkness into which I was born: sin and ignorance.
>
> You make eloquent the tongues of infants. Refine my speech and pour forth from my lips the goodness of Your blessing.
>
> Grant to me keenness of mind, capacity to remember, skill in learning, subtlety to interpret, and eloquence of speech.
>
> May you guide the beginning of my work, direct its progress, and bring it to completion.
>
> You Who are true God and true Man, Who lives and reigns, world without end. Amen.[21]

19. Goering, "Christ in Dominican Catechesis."
20. Healy, *Thomas Aquinas*, 33-34.
21. *The Aquinas Prayer Book: The Prayers and Hymns of St. Thomas Aquinas*, trans. and ed. Robert Anderson and Johann Moser (Manchester, NH: Sophia Institute Press, 2000), 41-43.

Working within the biblical culture cultivated by the Dominicans and other mendicant orders, Aquinas bore the title *magister in sacra pagina* ("master of the sacred page"), which refers to the entire effort of bearing witness to the revelation of the Word by the interpretive activity of Scripture that is its normative source. "His theology served his community and the preaching of the church as they and he sought to follow Christ more fittingly and obediently. Christians follow the way that is the incarnate Word of God. . . . The chief guide is the apostolic text."[22] These responsibilities were appropriately defined in the context of apostolic ministry where all three functions — doctrine, exegesis, and preaching — arose from the profession of theology *(theologia)*, or sacred doctrine *(sacra doctrina)*, the activity of passing on, or handing over, God's self-knowledge and love, which is wisdom, and derivative of the Son of God, the incarnate Word, through the witness of Scripture and workings of the Spirit.[23]

> These tasks, however, were not distinct disciplines as in modern practice; they were all seen as parts of a more or less unified theological program of articulating, shaping and embodying convictions about God, humanity and the world in order to communicate and nurture Christian wisdom. This ensemble of theological practices — exegetical, dogmatic and pastoral in nature — were personally integrated within a sapiential vision shaped by the Gospel; each of these required a receptivity, transmission, and participation evoked by the active presence of the Word and the operation of the Holy Spirit for its realization in the life of the church and the salvation of the world.[24]

The Summa Theologiae: *Theology for Preachers*

The most important work of Thomas Aquinas was the *Summa Theologiae* (ST), which must be understood within the context of his vocation as a Dominican, his study of Scripture and the church fathers, his engagement with philosophy and other forms of human knowledge,

22. Healy, *Thomas Aquinas,* 47.
23. Torrell, *Saint Thomas Aquinas,* 1.4-74.2.1-24.
24. Chenu, *Aquinas and His Role in Theology,* 20-31.

and his commitment to the Dominican Order's principles of obedience, poverty, and preaching.[25] The purpose of the *Summa* was the formation of Dominicans, both beginners and advanced students: to interpret Scripture and debate doctrinal matters in performing their vocation of teaching, preaching, and living the gospel more faithfully by following Christ.[26] As Thomas writes in the Prologue to *ST*, "Since the doctor of the Catholic truth must not only teach the most advanced but also instruct beginners . . . my intention is to explain what concerns the Christian religion in a way that is appropriate for the formation of beginners."

Thomas's concept of *sacra doctrina* ("holy teaching") reflects Dominic's original commitment to the mission of *sancta praedicatia* ("holy preaching"), which wisely adapted the expression of gospel truth to the capacities of listeners.[27] Francis Martin observes:

> *Sacra Doctrina,* the whole sweep of divine teaching and divinely sustained transmission of that teaching, includes in its heart a witness to and presence of the revealing and life-giving action of God in his Son Jesus Christ. . . . By extension, the term *sacra doctrina* applies to all the derivative human acts, initiated and sustained by the Holy Spirit, by which this originating activity is perpetuated and made available, in many forms [including preaching] to subsequent generations of God's people.[28]

It is significant that the narrative movement of the *Summa* depends on the literal sense of Scripture for its ordering: moving from God to creatures and to Christ, through whom all creatures return to God. "Exegesis of that story is thus a necessary part of all theological in-

---

25. Thomas Aquinas, *Summa Theologiae,* trans. Fathers of the English Dominican Province (Westminster, Md.: Christian Classics, 1981). (Hereafter, references to this source will appear in parentheses in the text.)

26. See the discussion in Kerr, *After Aquinas,* 117, 162-68.

27. Leonard Boyle, O.P., *The Setting of the* Summa Theologiae *of Thomas Aquinas* (Toronto: Pontifical Institute of Medieval Studies, 1981); Healy, *Thomas Aquinas,* 28-48; Nichols, *Discovering Aquinas,* 9-18; Kerr, *After Aquinas,* 117-19. See the excellent discussion of the *Summa* and its use in John I. Jenkins, C.S.C., *Knowledge and Faith in Thomas Aquinas* (Cambridge, UK: Cambridge University Press, 2001).

28. R. Francis Martin, "*Sacra Doctrina* and the Authority of Its *Sacra Scriptura,*" *Pro Ecclesia* 10, no. 1 (2000): 85.

quiry."[29] This is from first to last a narrative of the Word, as the wisdom of the Father who breathes forth all things through the Spirit as gift and love. The *Prima Pars* deals with God: both one and triune in himself as the source and goal of all creation. The *Secunda Pars* deals specifically with practical theology: the study of the Christian life, the drama of conversion and true discipleship, and the virtues and vices — the narrative of human beings called to achieve their restoration and renewal through knowing God and exercising human freedom with the empowerment of divine grace. The *Tertia Pars* provides the climax of the whole work in Christ, the Son of God, present in the incarnation and sacramental life of the church, the form of humanity's return to God through the grace of the Holy Spirit.[30] Nicholas Healy comments on this:

> For Thomas, Christianity is a way of life founded upon the assent of believers to what they have heard of God's revelation. That assent — faith — is made possible by the Holy Spirit and the preaching of the Church. Revelation is the necessary basis for Christianity because Christians are oriented to a goal that is beyond our natural capacities not only to attain, but even to know anything about. Our final goal is perfect knowledge of the triune God as we are brought to the Father in the Son through the Holy Spirit.[31]

The doctrine of the Trinity is at the heart of Thomas's theology. As Emery has shown, Thomas's teaching on the Trinity demonstrates that the triune God may be reasonably conceived, while also providing the basic structure of reality, of the world, and or history. In Emery's words, "Through the procession of the Son and of the Spirit, which is the cause and reason for the creation and return to God, the world created by the Father is brought back to the Father."[32]

Sacred doctrine engenders a contemplative wisdom patterned after

---

29. Nicholas M. Healy, "Introduction," in *Aquinas on Scripture,* ed. Thomas G. Weinandy, Daniel A. Keating, and John P. Yocum (London/New York: T&T Clark, 2005), 17.

30. Torrell, *Saint Thomas Aquinas,* vol. 2, *Spiritual Master,* 25-52; Nichols, *Discovering Thomas Aquinas,* 9-13;

31. Healy, "Introduction," in *Aquinas on Scripture,* 13.

32. Giles Emery, "The Doctrine of the Trinity in St. Thomas Aquinas," in *Aquinas on Doctrine,* ed. Thomas Weinandy, Daniel Keating, and John Yocum (London/New York: T&T Clark, 2004), 66-67.

the Christ-centered narrative of Scripture, a pedagogical process that serves the reading of Scripture to nurture participation in the revealing and saving activity of God; extending from God as creating to God as beatifying; in raising the dead, from creation to resurrection and to human flourishing in God. Christopher Baglow clarifies the unity of sacred Scripture and sacred doctrine within the broader dynamism of divine revelation.

> This is because the distinction between the two is much less important for Thomas than the fact that the two are derivative of the true center and source of all revelation — the divine Son of God. . . . [The] incarnational pattern described by [the Gospel of John] and wonderfully interpreted by Thomas is the analogy par excellence for the Thomistic notion of scriptural revelation: the fact that the words of Scripture are human words make them a way which the human mind can traverse; the fact that these human words contain divine revelation make them the medium of divine truth as well as salvation. . . . Just as Scripture follows and participates in the pattern of the Incarnation, so to break scriptural revelation away from later articulations would be parallel to a static separation of Christ's presence in human history in his life and death, and by his ongoing presence to the Church in his resurrection.[33]

As they unfold the pattern of divine revelation — God creating, saving, and perfecting — the first two parts of the *Summa* may be seen as an elaborate statement of the *dramatis personae,* God and humanity, with a supporting cast of other creatures.[34] This drama consists of bringing together God and us in beatitude, which is a happiness created by grace in loving communion, or friendship, with God. This drama centers on the Son, who reveals the wisdom of the Father's art, the model and objective foundation of our movement toward God. Thus the incarnate Word revealed in Jesus Christ is the way by which we are restored to the divine image as well as the Truth.[35] Joseph Warwrykow notes:

---

33. Christopher T. Baglow, "Sacred Scripture and Sacred Doctrine in Saint Thomas Aquinas," in Weinandy et al., *Aquinas on Doctrine,* 3, 12-13.

34. Tugwell, *Albert and Thomas,* 257.

35. Here I have followed the argument in Gilles Mongeau, S.J., "Aquinas's Spiritual Pedagogy," *Nova et Vetera* 2, no. 1 (Spring 2004): 91-114.

The end of the journey comes only in the next life, when the person is ushered into the immediate presence of God. God is the end of the journey. As ultimate Truth, God alone can fully fulfill the human's desire to know; as ultimate Good, God alone is the proper and fullest object of the human will. Life with God in heaven is, radically, a gift. There is nothing in the human person that can necessitate God setting God as the end of the person. Rather, God has freely established God as the end of the journey, inviting humans to come to share in God's own life of self-contemplation and love.[36]

The work of A. N. Williams demonstrates that the primary focus of the *Summa* is God — not "how" but "who" — and that Thomas is most interested in setting forth a theology that contemplates the union of God and the human being created in God's image.[37] Thomas thus renders intelligible for readers both who God is and who God has created us to be. Moreover, in leading us to Christ, Aquinas leads us to see the one in whom that union has taken place because of who the triune God is. His wisdom challenges dualistic notions separating the creator and human creatures, presenting their proper roles and integrity from the perspective of God's intentions, which are made inherent in us by the operation of divine grace engaging and enabling our human capacities (Williams, p. 56). Tugwell comments on this matter:

> [T]he immediate connection in Thomas' mind between existence and God is implicit in much of his theology, because it underlies his deep conviction that there can never be any separation between God and his creatures. The idea that God somehow "withdraws" in order to give his creatures space to be could never begin to make sense to Thomas; if God withdrew, then being is the last thing any creature could achieve. The freedom and inner consistency of creatures is not something that has to be defended against divine interference; it is precisely the gift that is made by the divine presence. The fact that things exist and act in their own right is the most telling indication

---

36. Joseph Wawrykow, "Aquinas on Isaiah," in Weinandy et al., *Aquinas on Scripture*, 46.

37. In this section I am following A. N. Williams, "Mystical Theology Redux: The Pattern of Aquinas' Summa Theologiae," *Modern Theology* 13, no. 1 (Jan. 1997): 53-75. (Hereafter, references to this essay will appear in parentheses in the text.)

that God is existing and acting in them. Without this fundamental conviction, Thomas would never have developed his doctrines of creation and providence and grace.[38]

Williams notes that, for Thomas, God has destined us for a union with himself that lies beyond our grasp, since to approach God is only possible through God and not by any other means. We are human creatures who, in creation, have come from God's eternal happiness in his triune being, and who, in redemption, are returning to the triune God as our eternal happiness with the blessed in heaven. Our salvation as human creatures, the flourishing of humanity, is found in neither ourselves nor the things of creation, but in being drawn to God in a union that begins imperfectly in this life and will be perfected in the next. And this is all because of divine grace, God's own self-giving, so that the joy it creates is none other than God himself and our participation in the divine goodness and happiness that God creates in us himself (Williams, pp. 60-61).

Williams's work is helpful in showing how the *Summa* unites theology and spirituality by engaging us in contemplation; that theological study, prayer, spiritual devotion, the exercise of the virtues, and the ministry of preaching are "ecstatic" or "eccentric" activities that emerge from and return us to contemplate God's nature and saving wisdom. It is in contemplation, or prayerful attention, that the whole person is elevated from a life centered in self to a God-centered life that alone is capable of satisfying human activity and desire. "The heart of mystical theology lies in the relationship between God and humanity, not from the perspective of what specifically human practices may foster right relatedness, but from the perspective of God's creative intentions for us. A mystical theology, thus of its nature integrates theological and spiritual concerns" (Williams, p. 56).

In both this life and the next our fullest happiness and well-being as human creatures is attained in a transformation flowing from, and leading to, the joy of knowing and loving God. The triune God is not useful for achieving human purposes; rather, God is the one in whose relationship our life is given as both a gift and the means of our sanctification in, through, and for himself. The practices of prayerful study,

---

38. Tugwell, "Introduction," in *Albert and Thomas,* 213.

loving devotion, and humble obedience transform and move us to live well in our return to God as the object of faith and satisfaction of the heart's desire, "the joy we associate with union with God, the bliss of paradise" (Williams, pp. 60-61).

In contrast to modern theological method (and homiletical practice), the theology of Thomas Aquinas is dominated by contemplation, thinking with love that joins the heart and mind to God, whose desire is to bring human creatures into face-to-face communion with himself: "One contemplates, not in order to make God welcome where he would otherwise not be, but in order to make oneself present before the face of transforming glory" (Williams, p. 69). Everything in the *Summa,* including the communicative dimension of theology, must be seen in light of this end: the participation of graced human beings in the life of the blessed in heaven. Study and prayer share the same goal and belong to the same charitable movement overflowing into an active life of teaching and preaching. Therefore, our conversation with God and with others is grounded in contemplating him. Of Thomas's spiritual pedagogy, Williams concludes: "We do not speak in order that others might be persuaded; we speak because we have been transformed to know and love God through the union of our minds with the Triune God" (Williams, p. 69).

For Aquinas, participation in the liturgical and sacramental life of the church immerses us in the proper means by which we enter into and proceed in this movement. As the true teacher of the church, Christ is also the measure of its doctrine, giving himself to the whole community in its performance of the story of his life, death, and resurrection that calls it into being. Doctrine displays the grammar of Christian discourse, a doing and saying given in Scripture that witnesses God's revealing and saving wisdom incarnate in Christ. This is "handed down" by the church through the preaching and teaching of Scripture, which is its authority (as sacred doctrine) and its content and activity (as teaching) and its source and context (as divine knowledge), engendering obedience to God's saving wisdom revealed and enacted in Christ.[39] Thus the truth we believe, love, and obey is Christ himself indwelling the church through the Spirit's grace.[40]

Dominican students of Christian doctrine immersed themselves daily in a scripturally informed way of following Christ that was given shape by liturgical and penitential practices. Gerald Loughlin says:

"Doctrine rests upon nothing other than the church's telling of Christ's story, upon the enacted reading, the non-identical repetition, of Christ's charitable practices, heeding the command to 'follow,' to do as he does; in short, upon the ecclesial tradition of discipleship." He continues:

> The story [of Jesus Christ] is known in the prayerful reading and performing of the [Gospel] narratives in the church's liturgies and common life. The story is known to piety, in and through the faithful practice of ecclesial life; learned through its telling in the sacramental and virtuous life of the community. It is above all a practical knowledge, *phronesis* rather than *theoria,* and doctrine is simply the rule and discipline of the practice.[41]

The Spirit's gifts of faith, hope, and love create the conditions for the church's performance of the scriptural narrative within an interpretive tradition by which the saving truth of Scripture is received and lived as its normative source and goal.[42] Within this movement — from God to humanity and humanity's return to God — human creatures are taken up by the wisdom of the divine teaching communicated in Scrip-

---

39. Healy, "Introduction," in Weinandy et al., *Aquinas on Scripture,* 15-17; Henrik Rikhof, "Thomas on the Church: Reflections on a Sermon," in Weinandy et al., *Aquinas on Doctrine,* 199-220.

40. Bruce Marshall observes: "This indwelling by grace of the one who is the truth itself, inseparable from the donation of the Spirit who is love itself, brings our intellect to the highest perfection it can enjoy in this life. The indwelling Christ gives us 'a kind of instruction by which the intellect bursts out in love's affection,' a taste of himself which is a 'certain experiential knowledge,' so that we might hold fast to what he says, to a truth we do not see. The name for this kind of knowledge is 'wisdom, a kind of knowledge by taste,' a wisdom which comes not first from learning, but from 'suffering divine things.' In the end, it seems that we believe the teaching of Scripture and creed not because reason gives us compelling grounds to do so, still less that we wish it merely were true, but because we have suffered the things of which it speaks." Marshall, "*Quod Scit Una Uetula:* Aquinas on the Nature of Theology," in *The Theology of Thomas Aquinas,* ed. Rik Van Nieuwenhove and Joseph Wawrykow (Notre Dame, IN: University of Notre Dame Press, 2005), 14.

41. Gerald Loughlin, "The Basis and Authority of Doctrine," in *The Cambridge Companion to Christian Doctrine,* ed. Colin E. Gunton (Cambridge, UK: Cambridge University Press, 1997), 54.

42. Kerr, *After Aquinas,* 162-67.

ture, thus transforming their capacities for hearing and speaking the Word by the power of divine grace: "We can think of the *Summa* as actually no more than a series of 'grammatical' notes, a guide for reading scripture, being entirely determined by the scriptural story of the world redeemed in Christ."[43] Jean-Pierre Torrell observes that God is the purpose of theology, which leads to the reality of which it speaks.

> Before all else, theology is an expression of a God-informed life, an activity in which the virtues of faith, hope, and charity are given full scope.... But it should be clear that this faith is not a pure intellectual adhesion to the collection of truths that occupy the theology. It is rather, in Saint Thomas as in the Bible, the living attachment of the whole person to the divine Reality to which the person is united through faith by means of the formulas that convey this Reality to us.[44]

Peter Candler's discussion of the *Summa* illuminates the wisdom of Thomas's theological instruction.[45] Following the pedagogy of the *Summa,* Candler argues for a "grammar of participation" in the life of God, a "curriculum of persuasion" that, for the Dominican Order, recommended a life of religious devotion as a "school of charity," a form of life in which one is trained "more perfectly to know and love, and hence, to be." As a "school of charity," the religious life is also a "school of memory," assuming a liturgical life by which human understanding and desire are ordered to God through Word and sacrament and centered in Jesus Christ (Candler, 138-39). "Remembrance of God consists not only in the recollection of an object, but points instead toward the

---

43. Loughlin, "The Basis and Authority of Doctrine," 45-57.

44. Torrell, *Saint Thomas Aquinas,* 2:4.

45. Peter M. Candler, Jr., *Theology, Rhetoric, Manuduction, or Reading Scripture Together on the Path to God* (Grand Rapids: Eerdmans, 2006). (Hereafter, references to this source will appear in parentheses in the text.) Candler concludes that the *Summa* provides an "itinerary of the soul," the fruit of a pedagogy by which the reader is not merely given information but is led into God: "That which holy teaching passes on leads one to beatitude, and the act of passing on this teaching is, for Aquinas, participation in the work of God in leading the intellect to himself. Therefore the object of the discursive *traditio* of the Church's teaching is at the same time to be led by the hand, which in turn is to participate in a procession of the Spirit to creatures, which again is coextensive with the return of the pilgrim city of God to its origin and end" (p. 132).

theological consummation of thought and desire in God, who is the proper object of both" (Candler, 37).

This theological enterprise proceeds in conversation with authoritative texts, the most important being Holy Scripture. But it is also a profoundly moral endeavor, a school of persuasion in which the prudential ordering of knowledge toward wisdom is a skill learned and mastered liturgically (Candler, 139, 141-45).

In describing the content and activity of sacred doctrine, Thomas uses a key term, *manuduction* (a "leading by the hand"), which makes the *Summa* a kind of "itinerary" by which readers are led by a master teacher toward the vision of God — "face to face." Both the intellect and will are led on this journey: the intellect directing the will, and the will moving the intellect, together being led by "intellectual desire" for God. Thomas's *Summa* "conducts" its students toward the *manuduction* of understanding and desire, a movement that is dependent on the agency of God by which "the will is being bent, and desire reordered, by divine charity, the gift of love, by God who moves all things to himself" (Candler, 105).

Training in "holy teaching" requires humility, disabused of human autonomy, and the cultivation of the virtue of practical wisdom, which judges and directs one's thoughts, actions, and words according to the wisdom incarnate in Christ. As a response to God's prior self-giving, the study of theology orders one's intentions, affections, and actions according to a wisdom that is acquired within the company of authorities "that participate in God to the extent that God consummates himself in a different manner to each of them. . . ." Within such conversations, participation in God's life is embodied in a "form of life" that makes Christians the kind of people they are through scripturally ordered memory, understanding, and will (Candler, 110-11). Knowledge of God is ordered according to a pattern by which we come to see that our origin and end is one and the same God, a "grammar of participation" that is inseparable from the language of Scripture and its liturgical enactment by the community of people whose story it tells.

For Thomas, the church is a community of interpretation, the movement of a pilgrim people toward its beginning and end, and a journey in which participants are also performers. Conformation of one's mind to God comes by cultivating habits of the mind and heart — the knower to what is known and the lover to what is loved — proceeding as an itinerary to the God who is both the teacher and the teaching. The goal, then, is for the reader to be persuaded to enter the school of charity — love of God for God's sake and love of the neighbor in God — through the "handing over" of sacred doctrine, a leading "by the hand" within a community committed to the gospel and the particular ways of living and speaking it creates (Candler, 125-29).

Healy similarly argues that Thomas's interpretation of the church is situated within an explication of the narrative of creation and redemption that seeks to demonstrate the coherence and reasonableness of Scripture in the authoritative tradition, or conversation, of its interpretation. By discussing the life of discipleship as obedience to the way of Jesus Christ, Aquinas sets forth a "practical ecclesiology . . . an account of what he believed to be the best thinking of his time about the beliefs, practices, and valuations that should be embodied in the concrete church . . . training and teaching its members to acquire those dispositions that orient them properly to their final end and so enable them to be truthful disciples."[46]

The art of living and speaking the gospel is engendered by liturgical activity that orders one's knowledge and love to God, a "grammar of participation" that derives its sense from ongoing performances of the Christian story of Scripture within a community of prayer, study, and discipleship.

> The claim is therefore that truth is not a possession of the church, but that, nevertheless, what the traditions of holy teaching hand over is true. It is not the case that the church "has" the truth; rather, it hands on the truth because its existence is a sacramental participation, though imperfect, in Truth. The distinction is subtle, though crucial. Though the language of theology is, as it were, derived from the language of the scriptures as these are learned in the liturgy . . . it is the performance of a vocabulary, and an interpretive enactment in the form of re-narration. In this sense, a grammar of participation distinguishes itself from one of representation by virtue of the role of time. (Candler, 39)

46. Nicholas M. Healy, *Church, World, and the Christian Life: Practical-Prophetic Ecclesiology* (Cambridge, UK: Cambridge University Press, 2000), 58; see also George Sabra, *Thomas Aquinas' Vision of the Church: Fundamentals of an Ecumenical Ecclesiology* (Mainz, Germany: Mattias-Grunewald Verlag, 1987).

The *Summa* unites the spiritual devotion of monastic culture with the intellectual pursuit of the universities to form an integrative expression of Christian wisdom serving the revealing and saving activity of God in its theological, evangelical, and pastoral dimensions.

> The truth about God such as reason could discover would only be known by a few and that after a long time, and with the admixture of many errors. Whereas man's whole salvation, which is in God, depends upon the knowledge of such truth. Therefore, in order that the salvation of men might be brought about fitly and surely, it was necessary that they should be taught divine truths by divine revelation. It was therefore necessary that, besides philosophical science built up by reason, there should be a sacred science learned through revelation. (*ST*, I.1)

Thomas identifies the principles of sacred doctrine with truths about God and God's saving works which God himself makes known through the teaching of Scripture to form the articles of the church's faith. "It is the Word of God incarnate who mediates God's *scientia*, or self-knowledge, to us sufficiently for our salvation. The witness to that Word is Scripture, *sacra doctrina.* And Scripture is to be read according to the first principles of theology found therein and brought together in the Creeds of the Christian Church."[47] The articles describe the center of scriptural witness as Jesus Christ, and situate him within the context of the whole, namely, the truth and goodness of God and God's actions revealed in the scriptural narrative of creation to the eschaton.[48]

It is via the love of this saving truth that God leads us to himself, eliciting a longing to understand what is believed. "As highest wisdom, it belongs to sacred doctrine to judge the truth of beliefs and the correctness of practice not simply in one area or another, but across the board. In just this way sacred doctrine is a participated likeness of God's own knowledge."[49] Therefore, "[t]he shape of the life of faith is its love for God and others, and it is precisely through this activity that the understanding itself is reformed and comes, by grace which has been present in it from the beginning, to participate in the full vision of God

---

47. Healy, *Thomas Aquinas,* 34-35.
48. Rowan Williams, *On Christian Theology* (Oxford: Blackwell, 1999), 47.
49. Marshall, *"Quod Scit Una Uetela,"* 15.

and God's life."[50] Nicholas Lash provides an elegant summary of this pedagogy:

> We might almost say that, for Aquinas, the "soundness" of his "educational method" depended upon the extent to which the movement of his exposition reflected the rhythm of God's own act and movement "outwards" from divine simplicity to the utterance of the Word and breathing of the Gift which God is, to the "overflowing" of God's goodness in the work of his creation *(Prima pars);* the "return" to God along that one way of the world's healing which is Christ *(Tertia pars);* and, because there lies across this movement the shadow of the mystery of sin, we find, between his treatment of the whence and whither, the "outgoing" and "return" of creaturely existence, the drama of conversion, of sin and virtue, of rejection or acceptance of God's grace *(Secunda pars).* And this, by way of explanation of how, in a summary of Christian theology Christ can make a central appearance only towards the end.[51]

According to the *Summa,* theological activity, which includes preaching the gospel, is not so much a human task as it is a form of divine self-giving and a primary way by which human creatures are drawn into loving fellowship with God. The communicative dimension of sacred doctrine, of which God is the principal agent, and the preaching and teaching of Scripture, as two of its expressions by human agents, may be seen as a divine gift, graced disposition, and fully human activity. Preaching is the fruit of the loving contemplation by which a preacher, impelled by the goodness of the Word and the Spirit's grace, proclaims the saving truth of God's knowledge and love in Jesus Christ.[52] "We do not draw close to the saving truth of which Christ speaks because we believe his words or those who are his witnesses; rather, we believe because we are 'of the truth' in that we have received the gift of God by which we believe and love the truth."[53]

50. Eric O. Springsted, *The Act of Faith: Christian Faith and the Moral Self* (Grand Rapids: Eerdmans, 2002), 175.

51. Nicholas Lash, *The Beginning and the End of 'Religion'* (Cambridge, UK: Cambridge University Press, 1996), 141-42.

52. On the importance of *habitus,* see Romanus Cessario, O.P., *The Moral Virtues and Theological Ethics* (Notre Dame, IN: University of Notre Dame Press, 1991), 34-44.

53. Marshall, *"Quod Scit Una Uetela,"* 14.

A Theological "Grammar" for Preachers

According to Thomas, the "preaching life" is a theological life that is engendered by contemplating God through prayerful study of Scripture, infused by divine grace, and transformed by the virtues of faith, hope, and love. Nurtured to maturity by the gifts of the Spirit, it follows Christ's way of evangelical beatitude leading to friendship with God and others.[54] In his reading of the Gospel narratives, Thomas interpreted the life and work of the Dominicans as a guild of preachers called to follow Jesus in the ministry of proclaiming and living the gospel and engaging the world in service to others.[55] As the fruit of prayerful attentiveness to God within the way of discipleship to Christ, preaching is a created or graced participation in God's own speaking and loving.

> The contemplative life is better than the active life that solely concerns itself with bodily necessities; but the active life that consists in passing on to others through preaching and teaching truths that have been contemplated is more perfect than the solely contemplative life, for it presupposes a plentitude of contemplation. That is why Christ chose a life of this type. (*ST* II.II.188.6; III.40.1-2)

The *Summa* can be read as an exemplification of contemplative fruit that nurtures Christian memory, understanding, and love, a "handing over" of sacred doctrine by means of holy teaching, living, and speaking. The movement of human creatures to God is the work of divine grace and the virtues that transform the intellect and will to know and love God, and thus to fully be (Candler, 127-29).

> First, as regards the intellect, man receives certain supernatural principles, which are held by means of a Divine light; these are the articles of faith, about which is faith. . . . Secondly, the will is directed to this end, both as to the movement of intention, which tends to that

---

54. Romanus Cessario, O.P., *Christian Faith and the Theological Life* (Washington, DC: Catholic University Press, 1996), 1-12, 103-24.

55. See the essays in *Christ Among the Medieval Dominicans: Presentations of Christ in the Texts and Images of the Order of Preachers,* ed. Kent Emery, Jr., and Joseph P. Wawrykow (Notre Dame, IN: University of Notre Dame Press, 1998); Healy, *Thomas Aquinas,* 28-32.

end as something attainable . . . and this pertains to hope, and as to a certain spiritual union, whereby the will is, so to speak, transformed into that end, and this belongs to charity. (*ST,* I.II.62.3 resp.)

The gift of love is central to the activity of theological judgment. As a quality given by the Holy Spirit, love requires not only knowing things about God, but also experiencing, receiving, or "suffering" divine things in sympathy with the divine realities known and believed (*ST,* II.II.2).

Although the contemplative life dwells essentially in the intellect, its origin is in the affections, since it is charity that draws us toward the contemplation of God. And because our end corresponds to our beginning, both the way and goal of the contemplative life will also be found in the affections. Our greatest joy is in gazing upon the beauty of the one whom we love, so that the delight we feel further inflames loving desire for the beloved (A. N. Williams, "Mystical Theology Redux," 63).

For Aquinas, to know God is to love God, while loving God brings about desire for a deeper and better kind of knowing. This begins with the gift of faith, intensifies through the gifts of the Holy Spirit, and brings an increase of understanding and affection that lead to practical judgment in obedience to Christ by one's speaking and acting.[56]

Healy argues that the missional context and concern of the *Summa* was to deepen its readers' understanding and appropriation of Christian doctrine by means of Scripture in following Jesus Christ, judging the content of preaching by their knowledge of him, and conforming to the character of his holiness in a life of humility, poverty, and love. "Theological inquiry's main function is to serve the preaching of the Gospel. And the preaching of the Gospel serves the Christian life, which

---

56. Gavin D'Costa notes: "This indwelling within love means that the Holy Spirit is properly present, guiding and leading all believers, including theologians [and preachers] into a deepening, indwelling with God, through increased knowledge (faith), through tireless struggle (hope), and most vitally, through the practice of charity (love). . . . Love thus plays this central part in Aquinas because of the three theological virtues of faith, hope, and charity. For Aquinas it is only love that endures, for in our final rest with God, faith and hope (which are always mediated in this life) are required no longer; for it is only through and with the love of God that we learn to love God and our neighbor properly." D'Costa, *Theology in the Public Square: Church, Academy and Nation* (London: Blackwell Publishing, 2005), 129.

is distinct from other ways of life, since it is an attempt to follow Jesus obediently."[57]

The integration of theological and missional purposes was especially critical in light of thirteenth-century conditions (as it is in our time), when popular, enthusiastic preachers were attracting large numbers of people but offering mistaken or misguided conceptions of Christian faith and life. The Dominicans approached preaching as inseparable from progressing in the Christian life, as constituting the movement of a preacher's soul toward God by service to others *and* strenuous intellectual activity: "Obedience to Christ's example is to support the preaching and teaching missions; it meant a life of study and intellectual inquiry in order to meet the intellectual challenges of the times by preaching the Christian Gospel in an intelligent and convincing way."[58]

For Aquinas, the life of the preacher is inseparable from the grammar of the gospel, which is oriented theoretically, practically, and experientially to the reality that is revealed by the scriptural witness and articles of faith that find their center in God's self-giving through the Son and Spirit.

> It is ordered toward the Triune God, as Christ's manner of life on earth was ordered to the Father in the Spirit. It is by his free obedience to the will of the Father, in the power and love of the Spirit, that the way to life in the Triune God is revealed to us and possible for us. The function of theology is to explicate the way of the Lord which serves the church in preaching the Gospel and forming its members [including its preachers] to follow it more fully.[59]

The spiritual pedagogy of St. Thomas provides a perspective from which we can better understand the wisdom and shape of the "preaching life" for our time. The narrative structure of the *Summa* leads us to know and follow Jesus Christ as our most perfect way into God. This journey begins with a consideration of God, as one and three, and a knowledge of how human beings reach God as their source and final end. This will require not only knowledge about God, but knowing and

---

57. Healy, *Thomas Aquinas,* 21.
58. Healy, *Thomas Aquinas,* 26.
59. Healy, *Thomas Aquinas,* 33.

loving God in himself, which is attained by participating in the person of the Word, God's wisdom incarnate, who is the content of theology (and preaching) and also its structuring principle. "Thus the consideration of Christ is seen to be the climax of a narrative of progress into God whereby the student of theology is transformed by divine wisdom and is thus enabled to preach and hear as one of the wise who participate in *sacra doctrina*."[60]

Furthermore, the theology of Aquinas embodies a mystical or spiritual dimension that is grounded in his contemplative approach to the mystery of the Trinity and of the incarnate Word of God. For both theological and spiritual reasons, the knowledge of God is sought for no reason other than God's beauty, goodness, and glory. This knowledge, moreover, is the fruit of God's own self-disclosure in creation and redemption. Through attentiveness to God and adherence to God's wisdom, we attain practical wisdom as well. It is in prayerful attention to God that our desires for relevance, immediate applicability, and usefulness are put to rest by the presence of God.[61]

Thomas's contemplative wisdom demonstrates the disposition of attentiveness and readiness to receive the Word of God through the obedience of faith and love, which is especially significant for those who preach and interpret the Word of God in the church. This vocation cannot be reduced to human sufficiency, strategy, or skill, since the essence of the Word we receive and proclaim is divine, and thus transcends human comprehension. "The only person whose witness sounds credible is one whose audience feels that he speaks from a sense of 'the charity of Christ which surpasses all knowledge.'"[62]

60. Mongeau, "Aquinas's Spiritual Pedagogy," 114, 112-13.

61. See Matthew Levering, *Scripture and Metaphysics: Aquinas and the Renewal of Trinitarian Theology* (Oxford: Blackwell, 2004), 238, 240.

62. Hans Urs von Balthasar, *Explorations in Theology, I: The Word Made Flesh*, trans. A. V. Littledale, with Alexander Dru (San Francisco: Ignatius, 1964), 237.

Homiletical Happiness:
The Joy of Preaching

A S A MASTER preacher and teacher whose primary interest was the formation of preachers, Thomas Aquinas unites in his work prayerful study with faithful obedience for proclaiming the gospel through faith in Christ and the grace of the Holy Spirit. Setting forth a compelling vision of the preaching life that is expressive of Christian wisdom, the *Summa* provides a God-centered, grace-filled pedagogy that is both contemplative and active, theological and practical.[1]

The *Summa* displays an integral but distinct relationship between God and human creatures that is dependent on the knowledge and love of God for its intelligibility, communicating the conviction that doctrine and ethics are inseparable within a theological framework of humanity's restoration to — and renewal in — the divine image. And while this unity is theological and intellectual, it is also ontological and dynamic in that it attempts "to reproduce the very movement of wisdom and the divine action in the work of creation — culminating in man the

---

1. Father Jean-Pierre Torrell observes: "Considered as practical knowledge (that is, theology as it directs Christian action — what is commonly called moral theology), theology does not lose its contemplative aim. . . . It is still and always directed by the consideration of God, since He is the end in view of which all decisions are made and the Good in connection with which all other goods [goals] are situated. To speak of God as beginning and end is not a purely theoretical option; it concerns the entire Christian life. If God is the source of all being and every being, he is also the accomplishment of all desires and of all actions." Jean-Pierre Torrell, O.P., *Saint Thomas Aquinas:* vol. 1, *The Person and His Work,* trans. Robert Royal (Washington, DC: The Catholic University Press, 1996), 157.

image of God — and in the work of divine government, which leads all creatures back to God their ultimate goal and happiness."[2]

Following the teaching of Scripture, especially the wisdom of John's Gospel, Thomas shows that the acts of the Word and Spirit as revealed in the incarnation and Pentecost, are extended to human creatures, which establishes a theological foundation for God's action in creation and redemption that unites God and human creatures by divine grace. This movement provides a theological principle for ordering human thoughts, desires, actions, and words Godward: through the processions of the Son and of the Spirit, who are the reason for creation and of the return to God, everything comes from the Father and returns to the Father.[3] In being drawn to know truth and love goodness, we are rendered conformable to Christ through the Spirit's grace, which engenders the joy of intelligent, loving contemplation of the Word and communicating its fruits in preaching.

The Christian life is one of joy, since loving and doing the good makes us happy. This happiness or joy is the fruit of delighting in God for God's own sake, and in acting virtuously for the sake of its inherent goodness, which is a participation in God's own happiness, or joy.[4] Fergus Kerr comments on the central matter of happiness as the true end of human life, a kind of "practical theology" that Thomas intended to situate between the mysteries of faith: the joy of participating in the triune life through the wisdom incarnate in the Word and the Spirit's gift of charity, which establishes loving friendship with God.

> In effect [Aquinas] sought to develop an ethos based not on obedience to this or that divine command, but in terms of the formation of the kind of person who appropriates and develops the gifts required for a moral life in view of the promised enjoyment of divine beatitude, a sovereign bliss which is God's own life. His interest is not in the rules we have to follow but in the kind of people we become, as we

---

2. Servais Pinckaers, O.P., *The Sources of Christian Ethics,* trans. Sr. Mary Thomas Noble, O.P. (Washington, DC: The Catholic University of America Press, 1995), 221.

3. Giles Emery, "The Doctrine of the Trinity in St. Thomas Aquinas," in *Aquinas on Doctrine,* ed. Thomas G. Weinandy, O.F.M., Cap., Daniel Keating, and John P. Yocum (London/New York: T&T Clark, 2004), 58-60.

4. Nicholas Healy, *Thomas Aquinas: Theologian of the Christian Life* (Aldershot, UK: Ashgate, 2005), 135.

practice this or that virtue or vice — of course in accordance with this or that expression of the divine law but principally in accomplishing the good which alone is our ultimate happiness.[5]

Thomas communicates a vision of God who has made human creatures for himself, constituting us in such a way that we will never be satisfied, or happy, except in the measure that we more and more deeply resemble the triune image as our true end. God has thus placed a desire — a need — in us to return to him, since our final and perfect beatitude can only consist in the vision of the divine essence, and we cannot be perfectly happy as long as there remains something of God to desire and seek. The whole of human life — intellectually, emotionally, and bodily — unfolds in desiring, embracing, and enjoying God as the source and goal of all human knowing and loving, the transformation of our capacities that leads to the divine image restored and our final end attained.[6] Or as Nicholas Lash puts it, "God is the object of our faith as the heart's desire, as the goal towards which all our life and thought is set."[7]

The origin of all this is the God who communicates his goodness with human beings who have been created to share his image. The means of this communication is a participation in the Son through the grace of the Holy Spirit, whose power engenders a new nature in Christ for a new way of living characterized principally by charity. This end orients the moral life of Christians, and it is the end of humans, the work of sanctification that has its primary source in the grace of Christ, who is both Son of God and, like us, truly human.

> To create belongs to God by reason of his being, and his being is identical to his essence, which in turn is common to the three Persons. We thus see that to create is not only fitting to one of the Persons, but is common to the whole Trinity. . . . Thus God the Father has produced the creatures through his Word, who is the Son, and through

---

5. Fergus Kerr, O.P., *After Aquinas: Versions of Thomism* (London: Blackwell Publishing, 2002), 118.

6. Here I am following the discussion in A. N. Williams, *The Ground of Union: Deification in Aquinas and Palamas* (Oxford: Oxford University Press, 1999), and Jean-Pierre Torrell, O.P., *Saint Thomas Aquinas:* vol. 2, *Spiritual Master,* trans. Robert Royal (Washington, DC: Catholic University of America Press, 2003), 82-88.

7. Nicholas Lash, *Believing Three Ways in One God* (Notre Dame, IN: University of Notre Dame Press, 1992), 20.

his Love, which is the Holy Spirit. It is in this way that the processions of Persons are the reason for the procession of the creatures in the measure as they include the essential attributes of knowledge and will (*ST,* 1a q. 45 a.6).

According to Thomas, the enjoyment of God, the happiness for which we are created to share, cannot be attained by external goods, possessions, or riches, either natural or manmade, since these are destined to *serve* human creatures rather than *rule* them. Neither can human honors obtain the fullness of happiness, nor do human fame, glory, or power. Thomas excludes these as external ends, along with the goals of life, health, and pleasure; he identifies them as goods that are to be enjoyed in seeking our truest good in God.[8] *Preach from joy to Joy*

Only God's happiness or beatitude is perfectly good and capable of entirely satisfying our human desire. The object of the human will is the universal good, while the object of the human intellect is universal truth. God alone is capable of satisfying human minds and hearts by communicating himself as perfect truth and good. For this reason, the person who desires to embrace a life of Christian virtue will live happily according to the norm of truth and goodness through which God has accomplished the salvation of human creatures by the incarnate Son and the gift of the Spirit.[9]

The *Summa* thus devotes significant attention to the restoration of the divine image by setting the study of human nature and acts within a theological framework created by the new law of the gospel. Following the narrative of salvation history, Thomas describes human creatures' resemblance of God, the way they imitate Christ as the way to salvation, and the degree to which they progress toward God in him. God's work in creation was to form human beings in his image by giving them the capacity to know and love him. The goal is that human creatures will be led to fuller participation in the perfection of the divine image by contemplating the Father, Son, and Holy Spirit.[10]

---

8. *ST,* I-II qq. 1-5. See the valuable discussion in D. Juvenal Merriel, C.O., "Trinitarian Anthropology," in *The Theology of Thomas Aquinas,* ed. Rik Van Nieuwenhove and Joseph Wawrykow (Notre Dame, IN: University of Notre Dame Press, 2005).

9. Romanus Cessario, O.P., *The Virtues, or The Examined Life* (New York and London: Continuum, 2002), 4-5.

10. Servais Pinckaers, O.P., *The Pinckaers Reader: Renewing Thomistic Moral The-*

Grace renders man conformable to God. Since one of the divine Persons has been sent to the soul by grace, it is necessary that the soul be conformed or assimilated to that Person through some gift of grace. Now, the Holy Spirit is Love: it is therefore the gift of charity that assimilates the soul to the Holy Spirit, because it is in terms of charity that we speak of the coming of the Holy Spirit. The Son, for his part, is the Word — and not just any word, but He who breathes love: "The Word that we try to make known," says Augustine, "is a complete understanding of love." The Son is not sent for just any perfecting of the intellect, but only where the intellect is instructed in such a way that it melts in the affection of love, as it is written in the Gospel of John (6:45): "Whoever has heard the Father and accepted his teaching comes to me," or in Psalm 38:4: "In my meditation a fire will be kindled" (*ST,* 1a q. 43 a. 5 ad 2).

The movement of human beings in response to the divine initiative is centered primarily in the intellect and will, human faculties inclining toward truth and goodness and flowing from our spiritual nature to order the thoughts, affections, and actions toward God. The activity of the intellect, which speaks and forms ideas, and the movement of the will, which acts in love, are united in deliberate choice for the freedom of excellence that conforms us to Christ through the Spirit's grace.[11] Aquinas follows a tradition that looks to the New Testament as its source (2 Pet. 1:3-4).

His divine power has given us everything needed for life and godliness, through the knowledge of him who called us to his own glory and goodness. Thus he has given us, through these things, his precious and very great promises, so that through them you may escape from the corruption that is in the world because of lust, and become participants in the divine nature.[12]

Only the mystery of grace is able to account for such radical change in human persons, just as grace is necessary for human creatures to at-

---

ology, ed. John Berkman and Craig Steven Titus, trans. Sr. Mary Thomas Noble, O.P., Craig Steven Titus, Michael Sherwin, O.P., and Hugh Connolly (Washington DC: The Catholic University of America Press, 2005), 130-43.

11. Williams, *Ground of Union,* 61-63.

12. See the excellent discussion in A. N. Williams, "Deification in the Summa Theologiae: A Structural Intepretation," *The Thomist* 61, no. 2 (Apr. 1997): 219-56.

tain their final end in the knowledge and likeness of God's glory — "face to face." This participation begins with our baptism and justification, pertains in our present state, and will only be completed in the resurrection and life to come.[13] Moreover, since the habits created by divine grace participate in God's knowing and loving by the procession of the Word spoken by the Father, and the procession of Love issuing from both, the life of grace replicates, although imperfectly, the image of the Trinitarian life indwelling human creatures.[14]

Since every creature comes from God, each human fulfills the requirement for being a true image of the Creator, which is inseparable from reflecting on Christ as the one who fully embodies "the image of the invisible God, the firstborn of all creation."[15]

> The first born of all creation [Christ] is the perfect image of God, perfectly realizing that of which he is the image, and so he is said to be "the image" quite simply, and never to be "after the image." But man is both said to be "the image," because of his likeness to the original and "after the image" because the likeness is imperfect (*ST,* 1 q. 93 a.1).

For Thomas, the image of God is the vital connection between his study of the work of God, human action, and morality as humanity's return to God. This, in turn, leads to the study of Christ, who in his humanity is the way to God, while in his divine person is the Word of God, the perfect image of the Father. Moreover, the image of God in humanity is dynamic, in that the processions of wisdom and love, as proces-

---

13. Pinckaers, "Ethics and the Image of God," in Berkman et al., *The Pinckaers Reader,* 132-40.

14. Following Aquinas, Nicholas Healy describes grace in the following way: "Grace is the action of the Triune God that brings us into relation with God that so transforms and perfects the created relation that we live a new life in the Risen Christ. Grace originates with, and remains entirely dependent upon, the person and work of Christ, but it is appropriated by us and works in us through the power of the Holy Spirit, who draws us to the Father in the Son. . . . The grace of Jesus Christ is therefore necessary for us to achieve our proper end." Healy, *Thomas Aquinas,* 111.

15. See the excellent discussion of the divine image in Romanus Cessario, O.P., *Christian Faith and the Theological Life* (Washington, DC: The Catholic University of America Press, 1996), 38-48.

sions of intellect and will, are mirrored in the structures of human existence by knowledge and affectivity. Through the gift of charity, God becomes the source and object of our understanding and affection, giving rise to the conception of words according to the intellect, and the procession of love according to the will. As the Word knows and the Spirit loves, so human creatures are bound to God through the unity of knowledge and love.[16]

> Now the Divine Persons are distinct from each other by reason of the procession of the Word from the Speaker, and the procession of Love connecting Both. But in our soul word cannot exist without actual thought. . . . Therefore, first and chiefly, the image of the Trinity is to be found in the acts of the soul, that is, inasmuch as from the knowledge which we possess, by actual thought we form an internal word; and thence break forth into love. (I.93.7 resp.)

Servais Pinckaers comments on the significance of Thomas's teaching on the interior source of the gospel, rather than exterior rules or obligations, which works to create a kind of "spiritual contemporaneity" from Pentecost to the present, "a living experience of the divine realities that are believed." For Thomas, the gospel is not only a historical word and exegetical subject, but by the illumination of the Spirit it becomes a present Word opening up a future centered in Christ, God's incarnate wisdom, who as the teacher of saving wisdom unites holy preaching with Scripture.[17] Eugene Rogers comments on the relationship of Scripture to Christ as God's own form:

> Sacred Scripture records God's form in the world, or God's objective claim through providence to render things God's witnesses, in four ways: in the life of Jesus Christ, (principal to the most important part of the literal or historical sense), in the way that God's history with Israel prefigures it (principal to the allegorical or typological sense), in the way it involves human creatures in the working out of Christ's form indwelling their hearts through faith (the moral or tropological sense), and in the way it anticipates for them the life of God, where

---

16. Williams, *Ground of Union*, 55-64; Merriel, "Trinitarian Anthropology," 137-38.

17. Pinckaers, *Sources of Christian Ethics*, 174-77.

their searching reaches its appointed end: the life, the searching, the end — one thing — that began in them (the analogical sense).[18]

The moral teaching of Thomas leads us back to the divine source where faith, hope, and love are created by the triune persons who invite and enable human creatures to become participants in the divine Trinitarian being.[19] This knowledge is based on a twofold interior foundation:

1) On the natural law, inscribed in the conscience of every person and formulated by the Decalogue in the setting of the Old Covenant;
2) On the evangelical law, written by the Holy Spirit on the human heart by means of faith in the person of Christ and defined as the grace of the Spirit operating through the gift of divine love — faith working through love.

For this reason, the law of the gospel is neither an abstract message nor an external law by virtue of its written form; rather, the gospel is a law internal to humans, originating in God's self-knowledge and self-love, which is mediated by the missions of the Word and Spirit. Drawing from the teachings of Scripture and of Augustine, Thomas defines the new law as "the message of the Holy Spirit in the souls of the faithful," which overflows in the joy of speaking and acting well. Moreover, this new law is an internal law by virtue of the grace of the Holy Spirit. It is made external in human life by means of our human capacities. Yet the source of the law of the gospel is the grace of the Spirit, who is its energy and works in and through justification, sanctification, forgiveness, and perfection.[20]

By situating the evangelical life within a framework of grace, Thomas focuses on the words of the gospel, especially the Sermon on the Mount, as the specific text of the new law, just as the Decalogue was for the old law. For Thomas, this use of "law" is different from the judi-

---

18. Eugene F. Rogers, Jr., *Thomas Aquinas and Karl Barth: Sacred Doctrine and the Natural Knowledge of God* (Notre Dame, IN: University of Notre Dame Press, 1995), 59.

19. Here I follow Pinckaers, "Ethics and the Image of God," in Berkman et al., *The Pinckaers Reader*, 130-43; see also Pinckaers, *The Sources of Christian Ethics*, 172-88.

20. Pinckaers, *Sources of Christian Ethics*, 177-78.

cial or obligatory association it has had in modern thinking; rather, law is a work of wisdom that engages the intelligence and moves the will to act as a source of light and a way of love.[21]

Thomas viewed the Sermon on the Mount as answering the question of human happiness. He considered the teaching of Christ, which regulates the interior acts of will, desire, and love according to the Spirit's grace, as the goal of contemplating and preaching evangelical truth (*ST,* I.II.69). Thomas also understood the Sermon on the Mount as inspiring Christians to imitate the holiness of the Teacher, becoming true lovers of Christ by following the way of beatitude in the light of divine wisdom. As the wisdom of God taking root in human life, Jesus' sermon illuminates the mind and heart through the Spirit's innermost workings, which radiate outward to order human words and actions according to the law of the gospel.[22]

In other words, in reorienting our hearts toward our final end and happiness, God gives us a new law, Jesus Christ, in his life, teaching, death, and resurrection, and in his continued presence and work in the church through the Holy Spirit. In being ruled by God's self-giving love, our passions and desires are reordered to desire their true fulfillment and happiness in God.[23]

In attributing the work of regeneration to the Holy Spirit, Thomas establishes that the Spirit-filled person will be conformed to Christ, since it is necessary that spiritual regeneration come through that by which we are remade in the image of the Son by receiving his Spirit. And because "faith comes by hearing," no one receives the grace of the Holy Spirit as a mere individual, but is joined by the Spirit's grace to the mystical body of believers who are united to Christ by faith and in love.[24]

---

21. See the helpful discussion of grace and morality in Aidan Nichols, *Discovering Aquinas: An Introduction to His Life, Work, and Influence* (Grand Rapids: Eerdmans, 2002), 91-109; Pinckaers, "Scripture and the Renewal of Moral Theology," in Berkman et al., *The Pinckaers Reader,* 46-63.

22. See Pinckaers's discussion of Thomas and the Sermon on the Mount, "Beatitude and Beatitudes in the *Summa Theologiae,*" in Berkman et al., *The Pinckaers Reader,* 115-29.

23. D. Stephen Long, *The Goodness of God: Theology, the Church, and Social Order* (Grand Rapids: Brazos Press, 2001), 107.

24. Matthew Levering, *Christ's Fulfillment of Torah and Temple: Salvation According to Thomas Aquinas* (Notre Dame, IN: University of Notre Dame Press, 2002), 93-94.

Aquinas's soteriological vision of the old and new law is "based upon Torah and Temple, interpreted in light of Christ." Salvation history consists in the perfection of the worship of God, culminating in eternal beatitude, a union of happiness and holiness, which is "the point of Divine Law, Old and New."[25]

According to Thomas, such action is a source of joy, the affect of acting gladly and wisely, and with ease and pleasure, so that the joy with which we speak witnesses to — and participates in — God's saving activity and is itself a way of knowing God's goodness. Torell comments:

> We are neither good nor virtuous if we do not find joy in acting well. To act or speak with joy is to do so with love so that we find delight in it. It is not sufficient to perform good acts and to say good things out of duty, obligation, or by following external rules; it must also be performed, done and said with joy and delight according to the norm of the gospel itself.[26]

It would be difficult to overestimate the emphasis Thomas places on spiritual joy as essential to the moral happiness extended through the missions of Christ and the Spirit: moral action is bound up with the highest forms of human activity and expressions of joy, pleasure, and delight (*ST*, I.II.27-28). Therefore, while the human emotions are necessary for human action, they are dependent on virtuous acts that are done in view of a person's end. Without such an integral place for the emotions, passions, and affections in moral action, we will be reduced to rationalism, voluntarism, and sensate knowledge. And if our primary concern is with establishing rules, laws, and obligations as guides for moral acts, the emotions will be reduced to mere sentiment and affect,

---

25. Levering observes: "Thus at the heart of Thomas' theology of salvation lies the narrative of Scripture — the fulfillment of Israel's Torah and Temple through the New Covenant in Jesus Christ, which demonstrates the integral wisdom of sacred doctrine, investigating the nature of the Trinity, Jesus Christ, and human salvation. Thus Christ's perfect fulfillment of the Torah (wisdom) and Temple (holiness) are made one in the missions of the Son and Spirit, reconciling God and humanity, and allowing human beings to share, by the grace of the Spirit, in Christ's own self-giving of loving obedience and praise to the Father." Levering, *Christ's Fulfillment of Torah and Temple*, 145.

26. Torrell, *Saint Thomas Aquinas*, 2:166-67.

detached from spiritual and moral reality and subordinated to self-indulgence and manipulation.[27]

Happiness is constituted by "joy of the truth," which surpasses sensate pleasure, utility, and sentimentality in generous openness and receptivity to the reality of God and others. The gift of friendship is received through the virtue of charity: God's love for us and the love by which we love God and neighbors, of which joy is both a present affect and sign of future perfection. And because charity orders the intellect and will to God, the joy of knowing the one who is loved impels us toward outward expressions of speech imitating the indwelling of the Word and Spirit. "Outward speech is ordered to signifying what is conceived in the heart" (*ST*, II.II.3.1).[28]

> Hence Augustine says: *The Word we speak of is knowledge with love.* Thus the Son is not sent in accordance with every, and any, kind of intellectual perfection, but according to intellectual illumination, which breaks forth into the affection of love. (*ST*, I.43.5 ad 2)

Thomas's discussion of the emotions, passions, and affections is grounded in the union of intellect and will and situated within his discussion of love, delight, and pleasure (*ST*, I.II.31). To speak of the emotions in this way ensures an integral place for sensate feeling within the whole of a life engendered by love through the interior law of the Spirit. At the same time, this creates a reciprocal link between bodily affectivity and spiritual joy in the knowledge of the Word, which proceeds from the mind and heart of the Father.[29] Robert Barron notes:

> Thomas is decidedly not trying to capture or define the divine; on the contrary, he is attempting to show us precisely how to avoid the temptation of such definition. He is demonstrating how the soul can be liberated in the act of surrendering to God who reveals himself as an unsurpassable and ecstatic power in Jesus Christ. Thus, the simple

27. Here I am following the discussion of Thomas by Pinckaers, "Reappropriating Aquinas's Account of the Passions," in Berkman et al., *The Pinckaers Reader*, 273-87.

28. Fr. Cessario (in *Christian Faith*, 123-25) provides a good discussion of confession that is impelled by the presence of the Word and Spirit.

29. Pinckaers, "Reappropriating Aquinas's Account of the Passions," in Berkman et al., *The Pinckaers Reader*, 285-86.

God is the one who captivates us and draws us out of ourselves; the God who is present in the world is the divine power that will not leave us alone, that insinuates itself into our blood and bones; the eternal God is the one who invites us into the ecstasy of being beyond time; the immutable God is the rock upon which we can build our lives; the God of knowledge and love is the spirit who searches us and knows us, who seeks us and will never abandon us. It is this all-embracing, all-entrancing, all-surrounding power that Thomas seeks to celebrate.[30]

Homiletical happiness is the joy of knowing and speaking the Word through the new law of the gospel in conformity to Christ through the Spirit's grace by faith working in love. Therefore, to know God truly and love God rightly, which begins in this life and is completed in the next, is the greatest of all joys. "Such is the experience of spiritual joy, from which St. Thomas drew his conception of beatitude and which becomes the capstone of his morality. It is a participation in God's beatitude and joy that has been revealed in Christ and communicated through the Holy Spirit."[31]

Speaking Virtuously

The organic nature of the *Summa* is especially helpful for understanding the preaching life because it does not separate the dogmatic from the moral. Leonard Boyle describes the practical teaching of Thomas, which is inseparable from the fuller Trinitarian framework of the whole *Summa*.

> [Thomas] gave that practical theology a setting not evident in Dominican circles before him. By prefacing the *Secunda* or "moral" part with a *Prima Pars* on God, Trinity, and Creation, and then rounding it off with a *Tertia Pars* on the Son of God, Incarnation, and the Sacraments, Thomas put practical theology — the study of the Christian life, its virtues and vices — in a full theological context. Christian morality, once and for all, was shown to be something more than a ques-

---

30. Robert Barron, *Thomas Aquinas: Spiritual Master* (New York: Crossroad, 1996), 108.

31. Pinckaers, "Reappropriating Aquinas's Account of the Passions," 286.

tion of straight ethical teaching of vices and virtues in isolation. Inasmuch as the person was an intelligent being who was master of himself and possessed of freedom of choice, he was in the image of God. To study human action is therefore to study the image of God and to operate on a theological plane. To study human action on a theological plane is to study it in relation to its beginning and end, God, and to the bridge between, Christ and his sacraments.[32]

Through the theological virtues of faith, hope, and love, the gifts of the Spirit, and the infused virtues of prudence, justice, courage, and self-control, God confers mastery over our actions, faculties, and bodies for the freedom of excellence by which the gospel is fulfilled in human life. Because Thomas's moral teaching is grounded in theological wisdom, an account of the "theological life" is required to understand how the whole person can be perfected by the wisdom and virtue of Christ. While salvation originates and is completed by God's gratuitous action, God's action respects the integrity of our human nature, illuminating its transformation through the virtues that are formed by charity and guided by wisdom.[33] Romanus Cessario describes the virtuous life:

> If by a truly virtuous life we mean to refer to a comprehensive account of the good and perfect life for men and women, then only charity can make this possible for each person. Only the theological virtue of charity ensures that everything a person does reaches the optimum expression of our human capacities. This view does not require that one implement a sharp and rigid distinction between grace and nature; rather it recognizes what every Christian must accept, namely that the justification of the sinner results only from God's gracious benevolence. The gift of grace perfects the human person so that he or she can reasonably expect to follow Jesus's command: "You, therefore, must be perfect, as your heavenly Father is perfect" (Matt. 5:48).[34]

In describing the way we participate in our restoration to the divine image, Thomas affirms the traditional pairing of the seven gifts of the

32. Leonard F. Boyle, O.P., "The Setting of the *Summa Theologiae* of St. Thomas Aquinas — Revisited," in *The Ethics of Aquinas,* ed. Stephen J. Pope (Washington, DC: Georgetown University Press, 2002), 7.

33. On the "theological life," see Cessario, *Christian Faith,* 1-12.

34. Cessario, *Christian Faith,* 2.

Spirit with the seven cardinal and theological virtues, while he also includes the Spirit's gifts, the evangelical beatitudes taught by Christ, and the fruits of the Spirit. Because the moral life is ordered to holiness, holy teaching is necessary to attain the proper end of human knowledge, desire, and action in conformity to Christ, whose goodness confirms faith, lifts up hope, and enkindles love. For this reason, training in wisdom and the virtues within the pedagogy of the church is the appropriate way through which human creatures are transformed to the image of God's holiness by participating in God's life.[35]

According to Thomas, knowledge of — and conformity to — this reality depends on the virtues that qualify the mind *and* heart for communion with God. The virtues function to energize, integrate, and direct our capacities so that everything about us is disposed to a final end of happiness in friendship with God. Rather than being mere expressions of "works righteousness," the virtues assume that the intellect and will are oriented toward understanding and desiring something that comes to us and can be known, loved, and received: the communication of God's truth and goodness revealed in the form of Jesus of Nazareth. Thomas O'Meara says:

> These missions — Incarnation in Jesus, and presence and incorporation by Word and Spirit in us — do not just establish a relationship or turn divine contacts on and off but produce a lasting effect in their believing recipients. The empowerment for this order is grace. That grace is not only a new relationship or a divine acceptance but a vital reality in the creature: not a transitory divine help but a principle for people living in and toward a special destiny.[36]

The moral vision of Thomas is realistic in that it considers the needs of sensible human beings who are living and being saved within the ordinary, everyday circumstances of the world. Primacy of place is given to describing a transformation of human creatures through faith in Christ and the Spirit's grace, and to the practicing of the virtues and

35. Cessario, *Christian Faith*, 2-9; Aidan Nichols, *Discovering Aquinas*, 91-109; Pinckaers, "The Role of Virtue in Moral Theology," in Berkman et al., *The Pinckaers Reader*, 288-303; Healy, *Thomas Aquinas*, 107-32.

36. Thomas F. O'Meara, O.P., "Virtues in the Theology of Thomas Aquinas," *Theological Studies* 58, no. 2 (June 1997): 260.

receptivity to the gifts that are fitting for, and mediated by, our human capacities.[37]

Because the whole Trinity is the source and end of human salvation, knowing and loving God will require training in the virtues that elevate and transform our human capacities to a measure fitting for their proper subject. However, only the persons of the Trinity acting together can establish the personal and proper relationship of a creature with the Father, Son, and Holy Spirit, the "divine indwelling" that believing in God, hoping in God, and, above all, loving God is able to accomplish.[38]

Therefore, if we locate the Christian life (including the preaching life) within a journey moving from nature to grace and to glory, we will need habits to remain constant in ordering our intentions, desires, and words to God as the source and goal of this calling. And since the divine end to which we are called exceeds us, we will need a principle of habit that also exceeds us, which is our need for divine grace, and which renders our hearts and minds receptive to the missions of the Word and Spirit in knowing and loving God.[39] St. Thomas says:

> Some habits are infused by God into man . . . because there are some habits which man is disposed to as end which exceed the proportion of human nature, namely, the ultimate and perfect happiness of man. . . . And since such habits need to be in proportion with that to which man is disposed by them, therefore it is necessary that those habits, which dispose us to their end, exceed the proportion of human nature. Wherefore such habits can never be in man except by Divine infusion, as is the case with all gratuitous virtues. (*ST,* I.II.51.4 resp.)

Thomas considered the empowerment of divine grace to be indispensable for a life of virtue created by the infusions of the Spirit working through human nature. Because our affections and passions have been damaged by sin, they must be healed, elevated, and reordered by God's grace: "Acknowledgement of sin, acceptance of God's forgiveness, and

37. Stephen J. Pope, "Overview of the Ethics of Thomas Aquinas," in Pope, *The Ethics of Aquinas,* 49-50.

38. Williams, *Ground of Union,* 72-74.

39. Torrell, *Saint Thomas Aquinas,* 2:326.

constant spiritual discipline provide the deepest religious bases for moral correctness."[40]

Working through the interior law of the gospel, the Spirit infuses the virtues that transform us to act freely, by the activity of God, and to respond wholeheartedly to Christ's call to holiness: "You, therefore, must be perfect as your heavenly Father is perfect" (Matt. 5:43-48).[41] Thus, by drawing us to a God-centered life, the Spirit grants us a part in the divine holiness that constitutes happiness for those who complete, according to the divine purpose, the pattern established by Christ in the new law of the gospel.[42]

Michael Sherwin comments on the importance Thomas assigned to the mediating role of Christ in elevating and restoring human creatures to the natural image of God:

> Christ is the author of our sanctification. It is solely the life, death and resurrection of Christ that pours God's healing grace upon us. We receive this grace through God's son made man, whose humanity grace filled and from which it flowed out to us. We cannot of ourselves attain grace, but only through Christ. Aquinas further underlines that Christ effects this sanctification in us through the action of the Holy Spirit. . . . We are to be conformed to Christ and thereby given a share in God's divine life. . . . The primary gift of grace is God himself. God becomes present with us in a new way.[43]

The teaching of Thomas integrates the intellectual, moral, spiritual, and sensual dimensions of human existence to orient readers toward a final end that participates in the life of Jesus Christ.[44] He extends the teaching on the missions of the Word and Spirit into the instruction on the new law of the gospel, identifying it as an interior indwelling through the Spirit's grace; and with his teaching on the intellectual and moral virtues, which order the intellect and will in Christian

---

40. Pope, "Overview of the Ethics of Thomas Aquinas," 49.

41. Cessario, *The Virtues,* 79.

42. Cessario, *Christian Faith,* 54-55.

43. Michael Sherwin, O.P., *By Knowledge and By Love: Charity and Knowledge in the Moral Theology of St. Thomas Aquinas* (Washington, DC: Catholic University of America Press, 2005), 125-26.

44. Pinckaers, *Sources of Christian Ethics,* 221-26.

living; and with his teaching on the Spirit's gifts, interior promptings that complete the action of the virtues for the joy of acting virtuously rather than any external penalty or reward.[45]

Shaped by the interior law of the gospel, the evangelical life is engendered by exercising the three theological virtues — faith, hope, and love — which energize and fulfill the intellectual and moral virtues — prudence, justice, fortitude, temperance — and are completed by the gifts and beatitudes. "A virtue is an 'operational habit,' a disposition towards a particular kind of action. Since the virtues are habits that move us to act, they are the means by which we move toward happiness."[46] And since the evangelical life participates in the messianic mission and grace of Christ, it will be assisted by the seven gifts of the Spirit (Isa. 11:2-3). About the fullness of Christian existence as shaped by grace through the wisdom of Scripture, the virtues, the Spirit's gifts and fruits, and the teaching of Jesus in the Sermon on the Mount, Fr. Cessario says:

> The inspired Word of God supplies an instruction, a Torah, that is quite detailed, and that in the interpretation given it by Jesus and his New Testament followers enjoys universal validity. While the Ten Commandments summarize the Old Testament Torah, the virtues of faith, hope, and love, the cardinal virtues and their facilitating gifts of the Spirit, as well as the differing gifts of ministry given to the members of the Body of Christ express the moral teaching of the sacred Scripture in its fullness. For the precepts of Scripture do not of themselves constitute a complete ethics apart from the virtues of character which they form and express. As Christ himself teaches, "A good tree brings forth good fruit."[47]

Aquinas constructed his moral teaching on the basis of the Spirit's work, allowing him to integrate the teaching on the intra-Trinitarian

---

45. Marie-Dominique Chenu, O.P., observes: "Moral theology is and remains, like the whole of theology, a science about divine life. It forfeits nothing of its high dignity when its proper object becomes this divine life expressed within my human acts. Moreover moral theology in no way gives way to a dualism of theory and praxis. It remains unified and unifying under the light of faith, which, in daily communion with the life of God, is the living truth of the gospel." Chenu, *Aquinas and His Role in Theology,* trans. Paul Philibert, O.P. (Collegeville, MN: Liturgical Press, 2002), 117.

46. Healy, *Thomas Aquinas,* 119-20.

47. Cessario, *The Virtues,* 10.

life, the temporal missions of the Son and Spirit, and his teaching on the virtues, gifts, beatitudes, and fruits that dispose us to act appropriately in response to the gifts of creation *and* salvation. "The virtues, both natural and supernatural, engage our human resources, because they operate according to a human mode (the active side). The gifts operate according to a divine mode (the receptive side). They perfect the virtues by enabling our acts to transcend natural human resources."[48]

Furthermore, the virtues are related to the Spirit's gifts, which dispose us to be immediately responsive to inspirations that empower us to think, act, and speak according to a higher measure than our natural capacities allow. Finally, the gospel beatitudes direct us on a particular way of acting that participates in the happiness that is our end: the vision of God attained in communion with Christ, who is believed, loved, and followed for his own sake by the grace communicated in the "conversation" of his life and teaching. Pinckaers observes: "Such is the loving Word, received in the faith that justifies, which engenders Christian morality through the grace of the Spirit, who sanctifies us in charity."[49]

The illumination of the Word and the inspirations of the Spirit are intimately related to virtuous thought, speech, and action. The virtue of faith is complemented by the Spirit's gifts of understanding and knowledge; the virtue of hope, by the gift of the fear of the Lord; the virtue of charity, by the gift of wisdom; the virtue of prudence, by the gift of counsel; the virtue of justice, by the gift of piety; the virtue of courage, by the gift of fortitude; and the virtue of temperance, by the gift of godly fear.[50]

Thomas derived his understanding of the theological virtues from Scripture's teaching on the radical change accomplished by Christ in every dimension of the human being incorporated into his body. These virtues have God as their object: they are infused in us only by God, and they are known because God reveals them in Scripture. The virtue of faith has an intellectual dimension, knowing God as the first truth, and an affective dimension, desiring the first truth as both the ultimate end and final good "by which eternal life has already begun in us." At the same time, "[k]nowledge in faith is ordered toward acquiring the truth

48. Cessario, *Christian Faith and the Theological Life,* 163-64.
49. Pinckaers, "Scripture and the Renewal of Moral Theology," in Berkman et al., *The Pinckaers Reader,* 63.
50. Cessario, *Christian Faith,* 162-80.

about God and his richness, so as to draw the believer into the communion of Trinitarian love." Moreover, the virtue of hope accompanies faith and directs the will to God as the final good by which "we dare to hope for nothing less then God himself." Finally, both faith and hope are ordered to the virtue of charity, which "unites us to God as our final end" — to perform all actions for the love of God and in friendship with God.[51]

It is important to note that Thomas's teachings on the theological virtues — faith, hope, and love — correspond to his teaching on the creed, which is the summary of Scripture's teaching (on faith, *ST,* II.II.1.1, 8-9); and the Lord's Prayer, which gives voice to the desire that impels us toward the possibility of divine beatitude (on hope, *ST,* II.II.17-20, 83); and the Decalogue and evangelical law, which is the action of the Spirit working through the virtues (on charity, *ST,* I.II.100-102; II.II.22-28).[52] The explication of the *Credo, Pater Noster,* and Decalogue correspond to the spiritual senses of Scripture: what to believe, what to desire, and what to love in a communion of friendship with God that is made possible by the outpouring of grace in the liturgical life of the church.[53]

> Charity signifies not only the love of God, but also a certain friendship with Him, which implies, beside love, a certain mutual return of love, together with mutual communion. . . . Now this fellowship of man with God, which consists in a certain familiar colloquy with Him, is begun here, in this life, by grace, but will be perfected in the future life, by glory; each of which things we hold by faith and hope. Wherefore just as friendship with a person would be impossible, if one disbelieved in, or despaired of, the possibility of their fellowship or familiar colloquy; so too, friendship with God, which is charity, is impossible without faith, so as to believe in this fellowship and colloquy with God and hope to attain this fellowship. Therefore charity is quite impossible without faith and hope. (*ST,* I.II.65.5 resp.)

---

51. Torrell, *Saint Thomas Aquinas,* 2:352.

52. See a description of preaching and the virtues in Cessario, *Christian Faith,* 1-9, 149-58; see also Cessario, *The Moral Virtues and Theological Ethics* (Notre Dame, IN: University of Notre Dame Press, 1991), 94-95.

53. See the discussions of Thomas's interpretation of Scripture in Healy, *Thomas Aquinas,* 41-47; Rogers, *Thomas Aquinas and Karl Barth,* 56-59.

Aquinas defines the virtuous life as a *theological* life, because it is one thing to acquire knowledge about God, while it is another thing to give our whole selves to God, or to be made holy. "Only by grace can the human creature become what God is; this transformation of human nature occurs originally and preeminently in the Incarnation of the divine Word."[54] As an expression of *theological faith,* the preaching life is engendered by *God* through constant, active, and virtuous engagement that is attentive to its source and goal.

Because the theological life is a transformed life, the wisdom of preaching is understood best as the content, fruit, and perfection of attending to God through prayerful study and virtuous living that spring from its principal source of union with Christ. "Treating the Christian life in terms of the virtues thus enables [Thomas] to develop his account of the new law of the Gospel.... Certainly preachers need virtues, but they need them — as do all Christians — in order to become the kind of person who can readily obey Christ as they turn to serve God and our neighbor."[55]

Aquinas links the attainment of happiness with following Christ and imitating his wisdom, since our growth in truth and goodness proceeds according to the measure by which we cultivate the virtues that conform us to him through prayer, study, and practice. As the mediator between God and humanity, Christ is the way of truth, salvation, and human flourishing, the source, way, and goal of all human goodness, virtue, and gifts. And since Christ is the principal cause of the church's life and mission, the efficacy of his grace, which is mediated by his humanity, sanctifies believers to move toward a more complete and fully Christian way of life.[56] All our good works and good words, to the extent that they are referable to God, will thus be infused with charity and conformed to Christ, who in his humanity recapitulates the entire pattern or "grammar" of human sanctification.[57]

Aquinas follows the teaching of Isaiah 11 in discussing the gifts as inspirations of the Spirit that move us in a godly direction. The gifts are

54. Cessario, *Christian Faith,* 48.

55. Healy, *Thomas Aquinas,* 154.

56. Cessario, *The Virtues,* 7-8.

57. Thomas S. Hibbs, *Virtue's Splendor: Wisdom, Prudence, and the Human Good* (New York: Fordham University Press, 2001), 200-222; A. N. Williams, *Ground of Union,* 159.

permanent dispositions that enable a receptivity to the Spirit, who penetrates the heart of human freedom, virtue, and will and grants a superior impulse uniting divine and human action (*ST,* I-II.68.1). These impartations elevate us beyond our human inclinations through the gifts of Christ's messianic ministry: wisdom, understanding, counsel, fortitude, knowledge, piety, and the fear of the Lord. By relating the seven gifts to the four cardinal virtues and three theological virtues, Aquinas situates the concerns of everyday Christian life and ministry within a framework illuminated by the teaching on the Trinity, the Word and Spirit, and the communion of the church. Fr. Cessario notes:

> The Holy Spirit — the Advocate and Comforter — points the believer beyond the restrictions of human inclination and judgment in matters that pertain to eternal life. This "leading" equals a kind of pedagogy in divine things. Aquinas helpfully compares the action of the Holy Spirit to a teacher who gradually leads one to appropriate a sure grasp of a particular discipline by providing moments of insight that elevate both its method and context.[58]

The Spirit works via charity to shape the character of Christians for action that is prompt and easy: following Christ and choosing the good can become "connatural" or "akin" to the believer within the friendship established by the Father through the Son with those made in his image.[59] The gifts thus bear an affinity to the universal call to holiness that is God's self-giving: "The Christian believer ordered by the gifts of the Holy Spirit both knows and understands that God loves us, not because we are good but because God is."[60] Moreover, as a taste of future glory, the Spirit's fruit anticipates the completion of human goodness in friendship with God: "charity, joy, peace, patience, kindness, goodness, generosity, gentleness, faithfulness, modesty, self-control, chastity" (Gal. 5).

> The principal action of the Holy Spirit, working in humanity on this foundation of the spiritual nature which constitutes the human person, does not reside in the gifts but in the chief elements of the Evan-

---

58. Cessario, *Christian Faith,* 167.
59. Cessario, *Christian Faith,* 168-69.
60. Cessario, *Christian Faith,* 180.

gelical Law, as Thomas defines it. . . . With the spiritual interiority of human beings as its point of departure, the action of the Holy Spirit penetrates and forms with its freedom what we might call the Christian head of the organism of the virtues: faith, hope, and charity. These receive the gifts of the Holy Spirit, but also assume the human virtues, chief of which is prudential discernment, the will to practice justice, courage, and mastery of one's sensibility and body (or temperance).[61]

As an exemplary witness to the law of the gospel, the preaching life is engendered by faith in Christ, directed by the theological virtues, prompted by the Spirit's gifts, given shape by the Beatitudes, and perfected by the fruit of the Spirit in personal communication with the Word.[62]

Dominican theologian Herbert McCabe compares God's self-communicative reality in the person and work of Jesus to the coming of a new language: "Jesus is the word, the language of God which comes to be language for man." McCabe continues: "Jesus Christ is himself the medium in which men will in the future communicate, he is the body in which we shall all be interrelated members . . . he is the language in which we shall express ourselves to each other in accordance with the promise and summons of the Father. Now this language, this medium of expression, this body which belongs to the future is made really present for us in the church."[63]

"Good" preaching will be the good work of good preachers who find joy in following Christ and proclaiming the gospel through the grace he freely gives. The origin and goal of all this is the triune God, who in his generous goodness desires to communicate the perfection of his goodness in an intensely intimate communion of knowledge and love.[64]

---

61. Pinckaers, *Sources of Christian Ethics,* 177.

62. Thomas Hibbs observes: "The God to whom we are to be united at the end of time is a community of persons in whom there is the most intimate communication of knowledge and love. God's being is indistinguishable from God's knowing, and both are inseparable from God's speaking and loving. Christ is the Word *(verbum),* and we are images of God precisely in the procession of the inner word, an articulation of our knowing and a basis of our loving." Hibbs, *Virtue's Splendor,* 178.

63. Herbert McCabe, O.P., *Law, Love and Language* (London and New York: Continuum, 1968) 129, 140-41.

64. Daniel A. Keating, "Justification, Sanctification, and Divinization in Thomas Aquinas," in Weinandy et al., *Aquinas on Doctrine* (London and New York:

Thus the redemption of creation — viewed theologically as coming from God and returning to God — is fulfilled by the missions of the Word and Spirit. These missions are carried forward by the church in its sacramental worship, handed down in the apostolic witness, and communicated by preachers who delight in God for God's sake and find pleasure in speaking the truth in love.[65]

As the exemplar who reveals God fully, Christ is the teacher, model, and source of power for a salvation that is not only moral but makes us participants in God's life and speech. "As the Word, he presides at the first creation of things; as Word Incarnate, he leads the return of humanity to God. . . . He is simultaneously the One after whom we are created and re-created but also the perfect incarnation of the virtues and therefore, as a consequence, the model offered to all those who call upon him, and whom they must freely follow and imitate."[66] *We speak because we have first been spoken.*

T&T Clark, 2004), 152-55; Matthew L. Lamb, "The Eschatology of St. Thomas," in Weinandy et al., *Aquinas on Doctrine,* 226.

65. Pinckaers, "Reappropriating Aquinas's Account of the Passions," in Berkman et al., *The Pinckaers Reader,* 285-86; Lamb, "The Eschatology of St. Thomas," 225.

66. Torrell, *Saint Thomas Aquinas,* 2:372.

Preaching as the
Practice of Wisdom

MY AIM in the previous chapters has been to show that the person
and the work of a preacher — "the preaching life" — is created
by, and continuous with, the self-communication of the triune God,
who calls, gathers, and builds up the church to be a truthful witness to
the gospel in particular times, places, and circumstances. Therefore,
our vocation as preachers is integral to our identity as human creatures
who are made and remade in God's image in that we achieve genuine
selfhood precisely as witnesses to Jesus Christ, living and speaking the
gospel truth about the union of God and humankind. "The Christian
God is found in Israel and Jesus. God refuses to be known apart from
our life in God, which means to be made part of God's speech lies at the
heart of the Christian understanding of God."[1]

However, the more the functional tasks and quantitative results are
seen as the primary purpose of pastoral ministry, the less pastors will
possess the virtue of practical wisdom for judging and speaking in ways
appropriate to building up the church to know God rightly and love God
truly. For this reason, recovering the "preaching life" will also require
cultivating a "way of knowing" that reorients our loves in conversation
with the Word, which is received into — and is communicated by — a

---

1. Stanley Hauerwas, *Performing the Faith: Bonhoeffer and the Practice of Nonviolence* (Grand Rapids: Brazos, 2004), 77. See also the discussion in Kevin Vanhoozer,
"Human Being, Individual and Social," in *The Cambridge Companion to Christian
Doctrine,* ed. Colin E. Gunton (Cambridge, UK: Cambridge University Press, 1997),
158-88.

preacher's way of living and speaking the truth of faith. Joe Jones describes this practical wisdom:

> Because faith is an intentional action, it is as much a knowing-how, as it is a knowing who, a knowing that, and a knowing what. Faith is knowing how to live within the distinctive discourses and practices of the faith; knowing how to love and praise God, to give thanks to God, to pray to God, and to witness lovingly to God for others. . . . In this sense, faith's knowings are also practical knowings. . . . This practical knowing of faith is faith as wisdom.[2]

In *Back to the Rough Ground,* Joseph Dunne provides an insightful discussion of practical wisdom that explores the instrumentalist approach to practice that frames objectives in advance, anticipates plans, controls the moves one will make, and then proceeds to evaluate both the activity and results in terms of "effectiveness."[3] Following the moral philosophy of Aristotle, Dunne argues persuasively that practice is irreducible to external techniques or methodical procedures, and that it requires a kind of nontechnical, personal, participatory, experienced, first-person knowing that cannot be framed in terms of detachment, universality, and control that, though presuming to be merely "practical," actually embodies a definite kind of theory in itself (pp. 1-30).

Dunne defines this type of activity as a kind of "making" specified by a maker who determines its end or goal in advance. "*Techne* then is the kind of knowledge possessed by an expert maker; it gives him a clear conception of the why and wherefore, the how and with what of the making process and enables him, through the capacity to offer a rational account of it, to preside over his activity with secure mastery" (p. 262). In contrast to the activity of making that proceeds by mastery and control for acting externally upon the raw material of one's work, Dunne discusses the shared activity of practice. Practices are conducted in public places in cooperation with others, with no ulterior pur-

---

2. Joe R. Jones, *A Grammar of the Christian Life: Systematic Explorations in Christian Life and Doctrine,* vol. 2 (Lanham, MD: Rowman & Littlefield, 2002), 527.

3. Joseph Dunne, *Back to the Rough Ground: Practical Judgment and the Lure of Technique* (Notre Dame, IN: University of Notre Dame Press, 1993). (Hereafter, references to this source will appear in parentheses in the text.)

pose or goals external to the practice itself, and with a view to no object or outcome detachable from the moral intentions, desires, qualities, and habits exemplified and formed by the wisdom of those experienced in the particular practice (pp. 272-73).

This definition of shared communal activity helps to illuminate Christian ways of knowing, such as worship, scriptural interpretation, preaching, pastoral ministry, and evangelization. As means of grace that have God as their source and goal, these activities are constitutive of Christian identity and a way of life that is demonstrated and realized by particular gifts, virtues, and excellences that have been valued by the church across time. Dunne interprets this kind of activity as the embodiment of *phronesis,* or practical knowledge, "knowledge in action" that is personal, interior, experienced, insightful, and committed.

> In questioning the attainability of technical mastery over these areas an alternative to the technicist picture has been developed. In this alternative picture, practical knowledge has been shown as a fruit which can grow only in the soil of a person's experience and character; apart from cultivation of this soil, there is no artifice for making it available in a way that would count. In exposing oneself to the kind of experience and acquiring the kind of character that will yield requisite knowledge, one is not the kind of epistemic subject that has been canonized by the modern tradition of philosophy. One is at the same time a feeling, expressing, and acting person; and one's knowledge is inseparable from one as such. (p. 359)

The difference between these two modes of activity helps to illuminate the importance of practical wisdom for the right ordering of a preacher's life and speech by the knowledge that is judgment. When preaching is reduced to a matter of following "how to" steps — the practical application of techniques to produce certain outcomes — it is limited to a form of knowledge possessed by a person belonging to a specialized craft, so that the identity of "preacher" is redefined from that of a personal witness belonging to a particular community to that of an "expert" whose understanding consists of following rules or procedures underlying the production of predetermined effects, or "effectiveness."

Dunne concludes that practical knowledge, as a way of knowing in action, represents a form of *kenosis,* or self-emptying,

... its divesting of itself of godlike notions and coming to accept that it cannot have and therefore must no longer aspire to a god's eye view of the human condition. And this movement away from detachment, sovereignty, and imperturbability has at the same time been a movement into and a taking upon itself the burdens of finitude, contingency, situatedness. In subverting the Cartesian subject, it has been reincarnating the real person in the world of history and language, actions and involvement with other people — and, of course, in his/her own affective and bodily being. (p. 374)

Craig Dykstra has also commented extensively on a tendency toward reducing Christian practices to universalistic and abstract "one size fits all" procedures, rather than cultivating the skills of living and speaking faithfully according to scriptural wisdom that is embodied by participatory, contingent, and communal ways of knowing tested by the wisdom of God and the wisdom of the church. Dykstra's discussion parallels that of Dunne: when practice is reduced to making something happen — a combination of knowledge, power, and the application of skills and techniques for producing desired outcomes and results — its nature will be understood technologically, individualistically, and ahistorically. What matters most in this kind of activity is the merely functional, which operates via cause-and-effect relationships and depends on its utility for attaining immediate ends rather than convictions and virtues that are intrinsic to the church's faith, identity, tradition, and wisdom.[4]

Hence, what is moral or good and what is practical or effective become separate issues, just as the faith of the preacher, the method of preaching, the content and context of preaching are divided and treated as discrete, unrelated matters in the pursuit of "effectiveness." In other words, the fidelity between speaker and words, between language and truth, and between language and deeds is lost.

Dykstra argues that this popular notion of practice, predicated on effectiveness in production rather than excellence of the whole person, will be left, in the end, with no practice (and no practitioners). If the practice that exists is reduced to mere technical routine or process with

4. Craig Dykstra, *Growing in the Life of Faith: Education in Christian Practices*, 2nd ed. (Louisville: Westminster John Knox, 2005), 53-83.

no point other than making for change, it will exclude both the practice and its participants from an ongoing history of knowledge, understanding, and love in which the distinctive truth, wisdom, and habits of the church and its way of life are handed on and learned.[5]

Thomas Aquinas's *Summa* serves as an exemplary guide to our understanding of how knowing and loving God engenders practical wisdom, since it provides "a clarifying simplification of Scripture for the sake of preaching or confessing, and a clarifying generalization of pastoral experience brought back under the science of Scripture, or the whole of theology."[6] Aquinas directs considerable attention to the virtue of prudence, which, in keeping with the truth and reality of things, is able to judge, arrange, and direct one's words and actions toward the most fitting of all ends: the fullness of communion or friendship with the triune God.[7] Thus is prudence committed to a pursuit of the good that is rooted in a definite ethos with its own favored dispositions and habits.[8]

As a way of "knowing the truth in action," prudence is sustained by good character, which enables discernment of the good for the sake of

---

5. Dykstra, *Growing in the Life of Faith,* 76-77; see also Dykstra, "Reconceiving Practice in Theological Inquiry and Education," in *Virtues and Practices in the Christian Tradition: Christian Ethics after MacIntyre,* ed. Nancy Murphey, Brad J. Kallenberg, and Mark Thiessen Nation (Harrisburg, PA: Trinity Press International, 1997), 164-73.

6. Mark D. Jordan, *Rewritten Theology: Aquinas After His Readers* (Oxford: Blackwell Publishing, 2006), 153.

7. See a good summary of Thomas's teaching on prudence in Romanus Cessario, O.P., *The Moral Virtues and Theological Ethics* (Notre Dame, IN: University of Notre Dame Press, 1991), 72-93; cf. James F. Keenan, S. J., "The Virtue of Prudence (ST, IIa IIae, qq. 47-56)," in *The Ethics of Aquinas,* ed. Stephen J. Pope (Washington, DC: Georgetown University Press, 2002), 259-71.

8. About the *Summa,* Peter M. Candler, Jr., says: "*Sacra doctrina* is, therefore, not a set body of teaching per se, but the wisdom of God which is the appropriate ordering of human knowledge to its proper end. Prudence is the virtue required of the one who would be wise and it is no accident that already in the very first question of the *Summa* we are given a hint of what will behoove us to practice in this science. It is, as Josef Pieper writes, the 'cause, root, mother, measure, precept, guide, and prototype of all ethical virtues; it acts in all of them, perfecting them to their true nature; all participate in it, and by virtue of this participation they are virtues.'" Candler, *Theology, Rhetoric, Manuduction, or Reading Scripture Together on the Path to God* (Grand Rapids: Eerdmans, 2006), 114-15.

doing good acts that are a source of joy: "[T]he good practitioner has been formed by a history of participation in the practice itself. His or her experience of serving the end, or *telos,* of the practice — and recurrently trying to discover what this concretely requires — has laid down certain dispositions of character that, through discipline and direction, enable and energize" (Dunne, p. 378).

A prudent or practically wise person will possess skills of deliberation, discernment, and decisiveness that make him or her capable of transforming knowledge of reality into virtuous speech and action.[9] "Prudence not only includes making the right decision, but also demands we carry out the decision. In this way prudence links the intellectual and moral virtues (knowing and doing). Moreover, prudence shapes the other moral virtues insofar as it enables the just person to act justly, the courageous person to act bravely, and the temperate person to act with self-control."[10]

Following Thomas's teaching on prudence, Michael Sherwin argues that every human act, if truly human, will be directed "by knowledge and by love." The love of God, which shapes practical judgment for speaking and acting wisely, is directed by the knowledge of God in assessing the circumstances of life and responding appropriately in the midst of them. Thus theological wisdom, the law of the gospel, and moral activity are united and directed by knowing and by loving.[11] The comments of

9. Josef Pieper observes: "Prudence, then, is the mold and mother of all the virtues, the circumspect and resolute shaping power of our minds which transforms knowledge of reality into realization of the good. It holds within itself the humility of silence, that is to say, of unbiased perception; the trueness-to-being of memory; the art of receiving counsel; alert, composed readiness for the unexpected. Prudence means the studied seriousness and, as it were, the filter of deliberation, and at the same time, the brave boldness to make final decisions. It means purity, straightforwardness, candor, and simplicity of character; it means standing superior to the utilitarian complexities of mere 'tactics.'" Pieper, *The Four Cardinal Virtues: Prudence,* trans. Richard and Clara Winston (Notre Dame, IN: University of Notre Dame Press, 1966), 22.

10. Michael Dauphinias and Matthew Levering, *Knowing the Love of Christ: An Introduction to the Theology of St. Thomas Aquinas* (Notre Dame, IN: University of Notre Dame Press, 2002), 57.

11. Michael Sherwin, O.P., *By Knowledge and By Love: Charity and Knowledge in the Moral Theology of St. Thomas Aquinas* (Washington, DC: Catholic University of America Press, 2005), 230-40.

Servais Pinckaers are helpful for understanding the difference between "technical finality," which is based on a strict ordering of "means to end," and "moral finality," which transcends utility and technique within the order of grace, wisdom, virtue, love, and friendship.

> The finality of which St. Thomas speaks is properly moral; it is quite different from [technical] finality in the order of usefulness, or the technical finality we generally think of. The latter, based on the relationship of means to end, abstracts from the nature of things to which it is applied in such a way that everything can become a means or an end, depending on how we view it in the order of utility. Moral finality, on the contrary, is based on the nature of things and discerns certain realities that can only be considered as ends and not as means. Notable among these are persons and moral qualities such as virtues. One cannot effectively attain virtues, become just, courageous, or truthful, if one does not know how to renounce direct utility and immediate pleasure out of love for justice or truth. Likewise, one does not truly love another person if one is not ready to sacrifice one's own interest or the pleasure of that person's presence out of love when the need arises. Such is the love of friendship, which surpasses interested love and is of another order.[12]

The indispensable nature of prudence for the moral life provides an alternative to the popular vision of the preacher as "Gnostic technician," since practical wisdom, as the fruit that grows in the soil of one's love and experience of God, is inseparable from the whole self as a thinking, feeling, expressing, and acting person. "In the end the guarantee of the trustworthiness of practical judgments and the validity of moral judgments lies not in any code but in the verdict of good, experienced, wise people" (Dunne, pp. 358-59). Such practiced wisdom cannot be the product of a body of generalized knowledge or truths, a set of principles and procedures, or a "method" that can be "applied" according to technical rationality and mastery for the "effective" achievement of predetermined outcomes. Dunne says:

12. Servais Pinckaers, O.P., *The Pinckaers Reader: Renewing Thomistic Moral Theology,* ed. John Berkman and Craig Steven Titus, trans. Sr. Mary Thomas Noble, O.P., Craig Steven Titus, Michael Sherwin, O.P., and Hugh Connolly (Washington, DC: Catholic University of America Press, 2005), 208-9.

To speak of "action" as well as (but not separate from) knowledge and expression is to advert to the network of undertakings within which one finds oneself — the unpredictability, open-endedness, and to the hazardousness of one's undertakings within this network — the unpredictability of what these undertakings set in train. No one is exempt from action in this sense (a sense which allows that speech often is action); it is through it that one discloses and achieves the unique identity that distinguishes one as a person; and at the same time it reveals the depth of one's interdependence with others. . . . When one's actions are not imposed on materials but are directed toward other persons . . . mastery is not attainable. One cannot determine in advance the efficacy of one's words and deeds. (p. 361)

In his discussion of Thomas, Sherwin concludes: "What we love has a role in shaping our judgments. It moves the intellect to engage in the process of practical reasoning, and can focus the intellect's attention upon certain objects instead of others because of the intensity of the love it has for those objects."[13] For reason to discover the right act to be done, here and now, love must be ordered wisely toward the practical good that is timely and appropriate. However, love ordered well will be directed toward God as its true end, while disordered love will be directed toward the self, to created things as their own ends, or as means to ends less than God. Prudence, then, is akin to "love discerning well" with the power of the intellect working through practical judgment, counsel, and direction. It is an insightfulness that directs one's reason, desire, and actions to the end of loving friendship with God.[14] Thomas observes:

Prudence is a virtue most necessary for a good life. For a good life consists in good deeds. Now in order to do good deeds, it matters not only what a man does, but also how he does it; to wit, that he do it from right choice and not merely from impulse or passion. And since choice is about things in reference to the end, rectitude of choice requires two things; namely, the due end, and something suitably ordained to that due end. . . . Consequently, an intellectual virtue is

13. Sherwin, *By Knowledge and By Love,* 102.
14. Sherwin, *By Knowledge and By Love,* 106-18.

needed in reason, to perfect the reason, and make it suitably affected towards things ordained to the end; and this virtue is prudence. Consequently, this prudence is a virtue necessary to lead a good life. (*ST,* I.II.57.5 resp.)

Because prudence is "love choosing wisely," it is at the service of human excellence, that is, loving the truth and desiring the good, which renders happy the person who knows, judges, speaks, and acts well.

> [P]rudence is a kind of practical wisdom receiving a new, profound light from faith and a higher strength from charity; which unites it to God and deepens its understanding of the neighbor. Furthermore, it is disposed through the gifts of counsel, understanding, and wisdom to correspond to the movements of the Holy Spirit. Thus enlightened and penetrated, prudence becomes capable of fulfilling its role as director of action according to the designs of God. Its intervention is indispensable, because by means of prudence the theological virtues, like the others, can be embodied in concrete action. Without it, even charity could not discern and follow the right path with precision.[15]

There can be no wisdom or virtue without the gift of charity, since the goal of moral discernment depends on knowing God through faith penetrated by love. Flowing from the will to the intellect, charity transforms prudence for knowing the right end and choosing the right means in conformity to that end. As John Mahoney points out, the wisdom of the gospel and the illumination of the Spirit are the key elements of the new law that inspired the prophets and apostles and moved the saints to act. Therefore, in addition to a union of the heart and mind with God, the virtue of practical wisdom requires moral skills that enable one to assess specific situations and transform theological knowledge into appropriate action: speaking or doing the right thing, for the right reason, in the right manner, for the right persons, and in the right circumstances.[16]

Mahoney concludes that judgments concerning what is good for

---

15. Pinckaers, "Conscience and Christian Tradition," in Berkman et al., *The Pinckaers Reader,* 332-33.

16. John Mahoney, S.J., *Seeking the Spirit: Essays in Moral and Pastoral Theology* (London: Sheed & Ward, 1982), 67-69.

human beings are best received from the wise rather than the foolish; that a lack of wisdom is caused by lack of charity; and that the love of God works in us so that we love God and others as participants in God's life, as friends of God, and as God's sons and daughters by the grace of adoption.[17]

The mark of practical wisdom is a life ordered by love for God and the neighbor through prayer and the virtues. The virtue of faith grants knowledge of divine revelation as articulated by the articles of faith (the creed) to engender the gift of wisdom that judges their truth according to the grammar of God's self-giving in Christ. "The unfolding of doctrine in the practices of the church — for it is both a doing and a saying — serves to enfold the church into the very life of God. Thus all theology is finally mystical, a habit or 'wisdom' given by the Spirit."[18] Moreover, the end of wisdom, as the gift that unites human being and acting, "is to let the primary action of God to spread out in us the divine being, the divine life."[19]

While the Holy Spirit bestows the gift of wisdom, the virtue of practical wisdom is indispensable for directing virtuous performances of the gospel that participate in — and are improvisations of — God's prior performance of the Word in Jesus Christ. Stanley Hauerwas and Jim Fodor put it this way:

> When Christians speak of the eternally performing God, a God who not only creates but redeems, they are not referring to some univocal Being but to Father, Son, and Spirit. Indeed, because the Christian God is Trinity and not Being, this makes all the difference to how the character of human actions is understood as participatory in, and thus derivative of, God's action. This is especially important if Jesus Christ is viewed as God's true and most defining act. Because Christ

17. Mahoney notes: "It is only the lack of wisdom . . . that can make what is good in itself appear foolish . . . and can make what is judged foolish by the wise appear wise to the foolish. . . . Since our life is oriented towards the enjoyment of God and is directed by grace as a sharing in God's nature, wisdom for us is not only concerned with knowledge of God . . . but also as directing human life according to human and also divine considerations." Mahoney, *Seeking the Spirit*, 89-90, 78-96.

18. Gerald Loughlin, "The Basis and Authority of Doctrine," in *The Cambridge Companion to Christian Doctrine*, 57.

19. Aidan Nichols, O.P., *Discovering Aquinas: An Introduction to His Life, Work, and Influence* (Grand Rapids: Eerdmans, 2002), 106.

is regarded by his followers as God's most memorable and excellent performance (complete, holy, and finally efficacious because inclusive of all difference), the implication is that Christian lives, too, can become "holy performances."[20]

The virtue of prudence lies at the heart of the preaching life, since without prudence we cannot speak in ways appropriate to becoming "holy performances." "Good" preaching communicates God's goodness for the common good of the church, which depends on "a wisdom embodied in lives, practices and communities through the continual improvising of life in the Spirit shaped according to the 'mind of Christ.'"[21]

The shape of the preaching life is thus directed by the gift of wisdom that is received through the attentiveness of faith in Christ and the Spirit's grace. In other words, "performance that is truly improvisatory requires the kind of attentiveness, attunement, and alertness traditionally associated with contemplative prayer. All of which is to say that the virtuoso is played even as she plays . . . likewise, language speaks the speaker as much as if not more than the speaker speaks the language."[22] The practice of wisdom requires ingenuity and flexibility relying on intelligence and thoughtfulness that are immediate and intuitive, a way of "seeing" that is tested through long experience of patient decision-making and good actions within the communion of love that is the church.[23] Cessario says:

> Prudence aims at shaping the character of Christian believers so that they can fully participate in the communion of charity that abides in the Church. In the moral life of each person, the virtue of prudence must both conform and be conformed; prudence must be conformed to moral wisdom, i.e., to all the human intelligence can learn about a given subject. Prudence also learns from divine truth. In turn, prudence conforms to human behavior, so that human action lies . . . in accord with right direction that the ends or goods of human

20. Stanley Hauerwas, with James Fodor, "Performing Faith: The Peaceable Rhetoric of God's Church," in *Performing the Faith,* 86.

21. David F. Ford, *Christian Wisdom: Desiring God and Learning in Love* (Cambridge, UK: Cambridge University Press, 2007), 7.

22. Hauerwas and Fodor, "Performing Faith," 81.

23. Romanus Cessario, O.P., *The Virtues, or The Examined Life* (London/New York: Continuum, 2002), 99-121.

nature stipulate. Prudence brings us into right conformity with the "thing" or *res,* with reality as God knows the world to be.[24]

Thomas's discussion of practical wisdom reflects an emphasis on the unity of human wisdom, virtue, and the will of God, the apprehension of an analogy between the workings of providence and the virtuous actions of prudent human beings.[25] And because the work of prudence puts right reason into emotion and desire, it will be completed by judgment that draws from all the virtues to act as the "eyes and ears" of human excellence.[26] "[T]he very grammar of faith points up to a vital sense in which theology is intrinsically performative. Word and deed are inseparable in the Christian life and practice; nevertheless, because word and action do not always or completely coincide, Christians have always been concerned about 'getting it right.'"[27] Pervading the whole of one's life, prudence is the capacity that judges rightly, integrating theological knowledge and the activity of preaching in virtuous performances of the gospel. Fr. Chenu comments:

> Having these transcendent convictions and being empowered by its hope for eternal happiness, prudence still follows its appropriate means and keeps to its task and its functional orientation. Its efficacy remains bound up with the ways and means of its practical knowledge. Neither divine nor human love dismantles its ways of acting or its resources. The gospel moves through it.[28]

Thomas's description of the relationship between wisdom and prudence highlights the importance of the linkage between the Word of God, the content of preaching, the person who preaches, those to whom she or he preaches, and the end or ends to which we preach. Thomas says:

> Since prudence is about human affairs, and wisdom about the Supreme Cause [God], it is impossible for prudence to be a greater vir-

24. Cessario, *The Virtues,* 114.

25. Fergus Kerr, O.P., *After Aquinas: Versions of Thomism* (London: Blackwell Publishing, 2002), 123.

26. Pinckaers, "Conscience and Christian Tradition,"332-33.

27. Hauerwas and Fodor, "Performing Faith," 82.

28. Marie-Dominique Chenu, O.P., *Aquinas and His Role in Theology,* trans. Paul Philibert, O.P. (Collegeville: Liturgical Press, 2002), 111.

tue than wisdom. . . . Wherefore, we must say . . . that prudence does not command wisdom, but vice versa: because 'the spiritual man judgeth all things; and he himself is judged by no man (1 Cor. 2:15). For prudence has no business with supreme matters which are the object of wisdom; but its command covers things directed to wisdom, viz., how men are to obtain wisdom. (*ST*, I.II.66.5 ad 1)

Following the discussion in the *Summa*, Fr. Chenu lists the following characteristics of prudence: memory of past experiences; an inner feeling or desire for a particular end or good; receptivity toward wise and more experienced persons; careful attention to circumstances; determined exploration and reasoning that possesses the consideration of future possibilities; the assessment of opportunities; taking care to avoid obstacles; good counsel from a reason that is well ordered; right judgment about particular actions; and a capacity for discerning conditions in which exceptions must be made.[29]

Prudence, then, is neither a mechanical art nor a technical skill, but is rather a capacity that links the intellectual and moral virtues for choosing good ends that are internal, or appropriate, to a particular moral activity such as preaching (i.e., receptivity to the Spirit's grace); attentiveness to, and praise of, God; the gifts of faith, hope, and love; the building up of the body of Christ according to the New Law of the gospel rather than external factors (e.g., cultural relevance, pragmatic effectiveness, institutional self-promotion/preservation, the preacher's program or particular social agenda). "The intellectual virtue of prudence is concerned with judging well among those means not only as effective for the end but also appropriate to me."[30]

"Good" preaching is the practice of wisdom that is cultivated by receptivity to God's incarnate wisdom revealed in the apostolic witness to Christ: a nonutilitarian way of speaking that awakens the church to faith, for knowing and loving God in ways that are timely and appropriate to building up the body of Christ.

> Clearly the horizon of prudence or the Christian conscience is as broad as the Gospel of the Kingdom of Heaven, which the apostles

---

29. Chenu, *Aquinas and His Role*, 121.

30. Herbert McCabe, *The Good Life: Ethics and the Pursuit of Happiness*, ed. Brian Davies, O.P. (London and New York: Continuum, 2005), 91.

were commissioned to preach to the whole world. This means, among other things, that while being entirely personal, Christian prudence cannot be constrained within the limits of an individual life . . . or focused on the self. It is called to open outward and to collaborate with God's plans for the church, to become an ecclesial prudence or conscience, whose work will consist in building up the Body of Christ in great affairs as well as small. . . .[31]

The collaboration of charity and prudence works to integrate one's thoughts, affections, and actions in imitating the second person of the Trinity, the incarnate Wisdom of God. "Charity unites the virtues by ordering them to God, our ultimate end and our complete beatitude. Prudence . . . takes up the other end . . . and governs each concrete action and fulfills its function of judging all the other virtues, including the theological ones."[32] Governed by prudence, the knowledge of faith is transformed into fitting performances of the Word by means of human words that direct the church's intentions, affections, and actions to the one who is the source and end of all things.[33]

The Beauty of the Preaching Life

"Good" preaching will be the fruit of attentiveness to the Word through the Spirit's grace by which we are transformed to know and speak the truth in love. Moreover, because this conversation is determined by its source and goal, its nature will be contemplative (rather than pragmatic, methodological, or utilitarian), an activity whereby the super-

31. Pinckaers, "Conscience and Christian Tradition," 333-34.
32. Pinckaers, "Conscience and Christian Tradition," 349.
33. Hibbs says this: "There is an inescapable reciprocity between understanding and loving in the Christian conception of the good life. Although the virtue of faith resides in the intellect, the object of faith is simultaneously the first truth of the good that is the 'end of all desires and actions. . . .' The reciprocity of contemplation and action is also evident in the connection between the theological virtues and the gifts of the Holy Spirit. The goal is union with a personal God. . . . The intimate connection between charity and the gift of wisdom is instructive. The gift of wisdom is the fruit of charity. . . . It empowers us to conduct life in light of divine truth. . . . Like prudence, charity efficaciously orders the whole of human life and integrates cognition and affection." Hibbs, Virtue's Splendor, 188-89.

abundant beauty of the Creator is manifested to creatures in the form of Jesus Christ. "The Incarnation, on which the good life is modeled, embraces temporality, embodiment, and contingency so as to manifest their beauty and goodness."[34]

Commenting on the work of Aquinas, Aidan Nichols describes the incarnation as the fleshly, visible appearing of the convergence, or fittingness, chosen by God for the work of salvation. "The Son is beauty as the Father's image, proportioned to, resplendent with the expressivity as his Word." The perception of Christ's beauty has important implications for understanding ourselves as human creatures who are being restored to God's image. "Thus what God does is fitting and well-suited for his wisdom and goodness, which, in turn, affects Thomas' description of re-creation, or the economy of redemption . . . the missions of the Son and Spirit, and the indwelling of the divine Trinity in the human soul by sanctifying grace."[35]

There is a reciprocal relationship between contemplation and preaching within the apostolic relation: it unites us to Christ and illumines our perception of the goodness of God displayed in him through the knowledge of experience. Healy observes that the early Dominicans supported their mission of preaching by living their lives in conformity to the events recorded in the lives of Jesus and the apostles.

> That illumination is given only as Scripture is read within the apostolic church, amidst those who participate in the life of Christ through grace and the Holy Spirit. Scripture was written or normatively interpreted by the apostles as the basis of their preaching. It is, so to speak, the church's textbook, the instrument by which we may be brought into the apostolic relation to Jesus.[36]

Because the humanity of Christ is truly fitting, or appropriate, we are able to perceive in him — at least partially — the fittingness, or convergence, between the Creator and human creatures.[37] By participating

---

34. Hibbs, *Virtue's Splendor,* 165, 178.

35. Aidan Nichols, O.P., *Redeeming Beauty: Soundings in Sacral Aesthetics* (Aldershot, UK: Ashgate, 2007), 11, 15.

36. Nicholas Healy, *Thomas Aquinas: Theologian of the Christian Life* (Aldershot, UK: Ashgate, 2003), 46.

37. Healy, *Thomas Aquinas,* 38-39.

in the activity of the incarnate Word through faith, hope, and love, and by mirroring the missions of the Word and Spirit, we are enabled to discern God's actions to the extent that our minds are gradually conformed to the mind of Christ. By assimilating the activity of human knowing to the mind of Christ, the Spirit illuminates the intellect and moves the will as instruments by which the Word is contemplated and communicated to build up the church in faith and love.[38]

As Healy notes, "[Thomas's] theology served his community and the preaching of the church as they and he sought to follow Christ more fittingly and obediently." Aquinas perceived this "fittingness" as extending to the whole creation, since the Word is the intelligibility of all things created by God. In being moved to know the incarnate Word, which is mediated by the apostolic witness and interpreted in light of the creed, it is possible to discern, if only partially, the appropriate relationship between divine and human activity and thus the "fittingness" of the Word and human words.[39]

The first principle of theological inquiry for preaching is the incarnation: God's saving activity that is made "fitting" in Christ by his manner of life, his nature, and his person. Christ's actions are morally exemplary, and when we are obedient to them we act fittingly, and by acting fittingly through his grace we become conformed to his humanity. As adopted sons and daughters in the Son, we live our lives as refashioned in the knowledge of the Father through the Spirit.[40] Fr. Cessario says:

> In sum, because Christ's humanity remains personally united with the divine Word, one of the Trinity, and as much as we are joined to Christ as members of one Body, our share in the divine life flows

38. Romanus Cessario, O.P., observes: "While the sole efficient cause of belief remains God himself, God provides, through the life and preaching of the Church, a whole series of dispositive efficient causes that render the person more suited for hearing the revealed message of salvation. To speak of persons as dispositive causes may appear to slight the particular human qualities that distinguish one person from another, but the opposite is actually true, for the notion of causality in this context simply means that God instrumentally uses everything in order to achieve a result that surpasses the abilities any single person possesses." Cessario, *Christian Faith and the Theological Life* (Washington, DC: The Catholic University of America Press, 1996), 152.

39. Healy, *Thomas Aquinas*, 46-47.

40. Healy, *Thomas Aquinas*, 38-39.

from God through Christ and from Christ to us. The humanity of Christ — conjoined to the divine Person of the Word and united with other human beings in virtue of a shared human nature — remains the instrumental cause of God's saving work: Christ's humanity is the instrument through which and by means of which God "moves" human beings toward their destiny of union with him.[41]

Because contemplation is rooted in the affections, the vision of God's beauty, which is communicated in the form of the Word, awakens desire to know the truth and love the good that is truly our greatest joy, "so that the intelligibility and assessment of faith are of one piece. . . . [T]he intelligibility (and hence the persuasiveness) of Christian faith springs not from independently formulated criteria, but from compelling renditions, faithful performances."[42] Preaching is happy, and thus compelling, when it participates in and proclaims the wisdom of God that is contemplated in the beauty and goodness of Christ.

The role of the incarnation in the contemplative life is significant because it offers a perception that is commensurate with the human mode of understanding, of the form of divine life. "In Christ, we see the beauty of the divine life, and our desire to participate in that life is thus inflamed. . . . The active life, or the good life, is ultimately an imitation of the second person of the Trinity, the incarnate Word of God, who manifests the splendor of the internal life of God."[43]

Thomas discovered this Christological principle in the meaning of Christ's mission. All of Christ's actions, especially his preaching and teaching, corresponded to the threefold intention of the incarnation: "to reveal the way of truth, to elevate human creatures from sin, and to grant access to God the Father" (*ST,* III. Prol.). Christ's public ministry was carried out in a circular movement, integrating prayer and fasting in the wilderness with being fully in the midst of people for preaching and teaching the truth, with the fullest and most powerful preaching being his suffering and sacrificial death on the cross.[44]

---

41. Cessario, *Christian Faith,* 21.

42. Hauerwas and Fodor, "Performing Faith," 78.

43. Hibbs, *Virtue's Splendor,* 200.

44. Ulrich Horst, O.P., "Christ: Exemplar Ordinis Fratrum Praedicantium," in *Christ Among the Medieval Dominicans,* ed. Kent Emery, Jr., and Joseph P. Wawrykow (Notre Dame, IN: University of Notre Dame Press, 1998), 263-65.

Following the call to preach the gospel will lead through "the wilderness and public life" into a ministry overflowing with an abundance of contemplation and a desire to communicate its fruit with others (*ST,* II.II.188). By contemplating the triune God, a union rooted in faith formed by love, the church achieves its practical mission of preaching the gospel by faithful and fitting engagement of the world.[45]

The internal link between charity and wisdom unites contemplation and preaching in a life that mixes attentiveness to the Word with proclaiming its grace, beauty, and goodness to others. In other words, "good" preaching flows from prayerful receptivity to the Word, through which the Spirit's grace infuses the preacher with delight in Christ's beauty, love for Christ's goodness, and joy in speaking the truth that is Christ. John Saward expresses it this way:

> Thomas has a theological aesthetic of grace. He does not forget that *gratia,* like *charis,* means loveliness and charm as well as gift and favor. Sanctifying grace is divinizing grace, a participation in the divine nature, a share in the life of the Triune God. Now the divine nature is beautiful; the Triune God is super-beauty; and so the divinized soul is divinely beautiful. "Beauty of soul consists in becoming like God." The saints owe everything to Christ. They are men and women in whom His divinizing, beautifying grace is more resplendent. They are the Father's great work of art, human beings who have let the Holy Spirit purge and fashion them into the likeness of the incarnate Son, changed from glory to glory. Their souls . . . have a "Christed beauty."[46]

By directing attention to the beauty and goodness of human creatures in their relationship to the incarnate Word in whom they have

---

45. In this connection, Hauerwas and Fodor note: "Patient listening and attentiveness are skills that are exercised, honed, and refined in Christian communities. Moreover, within the life of the church this type of respectful attentive listening is acquired primarily in the liturgy: this is where Christians learn . . . 'repentant attention' — reverence toward one another and receptivity to God. Attentive listening cannot be had without two inseparable companions — obedience and patience. Indeed, Christians must be instructed in patience as well as in action, for patience forms a part of all true action." Hauerwas and Fodor, "Performing Faith," 100.

46. John Saward, *The Beauty of Holiness and the Holiness of Beauty: Art, Sanctity and the Truth of Catholicism* (San Francisco: Ignatius Press, 1996), 62-63.

been fashioned and are refashioned, Thomas transcends utilitarian and instrumental notions that separate the beautiful from the good, reduce the truthful life to self-sufficiency, and limit the moral life to technique.[47] Or to put this in a different way, we need a sense of beauty to know and love God, since without beauty the true and the good are subject to instrumentality: knowing the truth becomes programmatic and formalistic, desire for the good becomes utilitarian and hedonistic, and their value is reduced to necessity and efficiency.[48] Thomas presents an alternative vision:

> Consequently, the contemplative life, as regards the essence of the action, pertains to the intellect, but as regards the motive cause of the exercise of that action it belongs to the will, which moves all the other powers, even the intellect, to their actions. . . . Wherefore Gregory makes the contemplative life to consist in the love of God, inasmuch as through loving God we are aflame to gaze on His beauty. And since everyone delights when he obtains what he loves, it follows that the contemplative life terminates in delight, which is seated in the affective power, the result being that love also becomes more intense. (*ST,* II.II.180 resp. 1)

Contemplation suffuses human reason and passion with wisdom and love, "an excellence or beauty that is shaped by God's excellence, nurtured by the new life in Christ to which we are called in the power of the Holy Spirit."[49] As capacities for acting freely and for excellence, the virtues restore Christ's beauty to the human soul, awakening the intellect to know the truth and moving the will to love what is known. Preaching is an "ecstatic" activity by which a preacher's whole intellect, will, emotions, and senses are taken up by God's self-giving into the joy of speaking the Word.[50]

---

47. Hibbs, *Virtue's Splendor,* 198-205.

48. Edward T. Oakes, S.J., "The Apologetics of Beauty," in *The Beauty of God: Theology and the Arts,* ed. Daniel J. Treier, Mark Husbands, and Roger Lundin (Downers Grove, IL: IVP Academic, 2007), 214-15.

49. L. Gregory Jones and Kevin R. Armstrong, *Resurrecting Excellence: Shaping Faithful Christian Ministry* (Grand Rapids: Eerdmans, 2006), 21.

50. Hauerwas and Fodor observe: "One of the traits of faithful performance is the way in which the performer is drawn out of him- or herself and is 'possessed' or 'taken over' by the work. This ability to let go of oneself, to dispossess oneself in the

Robert Barron has shown that, for Thomas, human ecstasy is awakened by the beauty of God's ecstatic, out-going love for creation as "other." The incarnation of the Word evokes a response of self-transcendence in those who see it and take it in, "an ecstatic way of being" with respect to the virtues of faith, hope, and love. The virtue of faith, which is an ecstasy of the mind, is moved to full expression because, in Christ, God himself speaks through a human mind and voice. The virtue of hope, which is an ecstasy of the spirit, is brought to full expression by means of appreciation and delight in just how much God has identified with us. The virtue of love, which is an ecstasy of the will, is "maximally excited" by God's total and generous act of love. "God's gift of self awakens a human gift of self, and the two together constitute a co-inherence of divinity and humanity."[51]

Aquinas perceived the whole creation as an artifact reflecting the divine art as the abundant, generous, and extravagant outpouring of God's love, wisdom, goodness, and beauty. In considering creation and providence, Thomas drew analogies to the work of artistic production, perceiving the divine artwork as a historical narrative centering in the dramatic encounter between God and humanity in the incarnate Son who is the Father's art (*ST,* I.II.93.1). As the Father's "art," Christ recreates human creatures to mirror the beauty of the Word by knowing and speaking the truth that is loved. "When we speak intelligently and intelligibly, the light of the mind shines through our words to give them clarity. If our thinking is clear, so are our words."[52]

---

very execution of the act, is a skill that is not learned quickly or easily and certainly not one's own. Indeed, if it is acquired at all, it is learned in communion and fellowship with others over the course of an entire Christian life. The power of performance, then, originates not so much in the performer but in his or her attunement to the work that is being performed, worked out, through and by the performer. . . . In this sense, true performance takes us out of ourselves *(ekstasis)* only to return us to ourselves fuller, richer, more deeply changed." Hauerwas and Fodor, "Performing Faith," 101.

51. Robert Barron, *The Priority of Christ: Toward a Postliberal Catholicism* (Grand Rapids: Brazos, 2007), 59-60; cf. Peter A. Kwasniewski, "Golden Straw: St. Thomas and the Ecstatic Practice of Theology," *Nova et Vetera* 2, no. 1 (Spring 2004): 61-90. "*Sacra doctrina,* or knowledge revealed by God, is necessary because the final goal of life is not to grasp but to be grasped, not to rise up but to be raised up, not to ascend but to be drawn" (p. 86).

52. Saward, *The Beauty of Holiness,* 51.

Because the source and end of life is revealed in the incarnate Word who has been spoken by the Father through the gift of the Spirit, the beauty of the preaching life shines forth as an offering of praise to God that participates in the goodness of the one who is loved and adored. As Hauerwas says, such simplicity will be a hopeful sign, "as Christians rediscover the beauty of the language necessary to praise the God who has gifted us through the Spirit of his Son."[53]

Seen in the light of God's refashioning work, the "art of preaching" embodies a way of speaking that imitates the beauty of holiness displayed in saintly lives and sacred arts in different ways. This is uniquely true of the divine artistry inscribed in the narratives of Scripture, which possess the character of saving wisdom and bear eloquent witness to God's act in Christ, the theo-logic, or "grammar," of God that compels us to join in the story of his life.[54] "The story is known to piety, the faithful practice of ecclesial life; learned through its telling in the sacramental and virtuous life of the community."[55] Hauerwas and Fodor say this about the grammar of performance:

> If the Christian faith from start to finish is a performance, it is only because Christians worship a God who is pure act, an eternally performing God. Trinity and creation are the language Christians use to speak of this God. . . . The Christian God is found in Israel and Jesus. God refused to be known apart from our life in God, which means that to be made part of God's speech lies at the heart of the Christian understanding of God. In short, our God is a performing God who has invited us to join in the performance of God's life.[56]

As a practiced "art," preaching imitates the beauty of Christ through the goodness of a preacher's whole manner of life, or "conversation" — intentions, affections, desires, actions, and words — which exemplifies

---

53. Stanley Hauerwas, "Foreword," in *Heresies and How to Avoid Them: Why It Matters What Christians Believe,* ed. Ben Quash and Michael Ward (Peabody, MA: Hendrickson, 2007), xi.

54. James Patout Burns, "Delighting the Spirit: Augustine's Practice of Figurative Interpretation," in *De Doctrina Christiana: A Classic of Western Interpretation,* ed. W. H. Arnold and Pamela Bright (Notre Dame, IN: University of Notre Dame Press, 1995), 189-92.

55. Loughlin, "The Basis and Authority of Doctrine," 54.

56. Hauerwas and Fodor, "Performing Faith," 77.

"the capacity, the eyes and ears to hear and mouths to speak, to discern the work of God in the world."[57] As both the center of the Christian narrative and exemplar of the Christian life, the incarnate Word illuminates understanding, enkindles desire, and orders speech according to God's providential work and wisdom, "[which] at its heart, has to do with the conviction that our lives and our world constitute a coherent story, a drama, in which God and humankind, together, drive the story toward its proper conclusion."[58]

As art honored in its use, preaching serves the church by imitating the beauty of the apostolic witness to God's goodness in creating and redeeming all things in Jesus Christ.[59] "Service is the art of the commonplace, the art that willingly enters into life with others and the earth and seeks the flourishing of all. The labor of art, which here stands in contrast to reductive, instrumental tendencies implicit in the desire to explain and control, seeks to expand our vision, and makes it more faithful to the mystery and grace that comprehends and sustains us all."[60]

Nichols describes Thomas as "a theologian of evangelical beauty, portraying the relation of the human person, the imago Dei, to God, the exemplar Source, as coming about by way of Christ's humanity and ministry which places the matter of fittingness, proportion, and well-suitedness at revelation's divine-human core."[61] Christian wisdom is the fruit of desiring God and loving wisely, which orients our vision to

---

57. Jones and Armstrong, *Resurrecting Excellence,* 19.

58. Scott Bader-Saye, *Following Jesus in a Culture of Fear* (Grand Rapids: Brazos, 2007), 79.

59. Paul J. Waddell describes the connection of practical wisdom and action within the narrative of God: "Furthermore, if Christians are called to carry on the story of God that comes to us in Jesus, a Christian account of prudence will connect wisdom about doing with actions that make the reign of God possible. How we finally determine what is prudent is informed by the narrative or story that most governs our lives. . . . For those trying to be faithful to the story of God, what might seem recklessly imprudent to others (e.g., a commitment to nonviolence, the practice of forgiveness) is eminently reasonable because it shares in and furthers God's ways with the world." Waddell, *Happiness and the Christian Moral Life: An Introduction to Christian Ethics* (Lanham, MD: Rowman & Littlefield, 2008), 190.

60. Norman Wirzba, "Introduction," in *The Art of the Commonplace: The Agrarian Essays of Wendell Berry* (Washington, DC: Shoemaker & Hoard, 2002), xvi.

61. Nichols, *Redeeming Beauty,* 16.

perceive the goodness of Christ, who in his divinity is worshiped as the truth of God and in his humanity is the way to God.[62]

As exemplar and exemplum, divine Word and human flesh, Christ manifests the truth of God in the story of his life, death, resurrection, and exaltation. By contemplating Christ with our whole being and all our senses, we can have lives that begin to reflect, if only partially and dimly, the beauty of his goodness in the habits of truthful speech. Hauerwas observes:

> Perhaps no place are beauty and goodness more united than in the truthful speech liturgy requires. The language of prayer is exacting, an exactness that fosters over time — elegance. The prayers of the church, unlike our prayers, have been honed to say no more and no less than what must be said to confess sin, to praise God, to respond with thanksgiving to the gift of Eucharist. Liturgy is the source of the word — care necessary for our lives to be beautiful and good — beautiful and good because by constant repetition we have learned the habits necessary to speak truthfully. To learn to speak truthfully is a skill never finished if we are to resist the lies that lie in the languages that speak us.[63]

Liturgy is thus the act by which "we participate in Christ, the humility of God, and thereby render God what is due to him, reestablishing the right order between Creator and creature."[64] The virtue of truthfulness flourishes in communities whose life is constituted by the apostolic relationship to Christ that makes us friends with God through the practices of prayer and the virtues, especially the virtue of truth. "Such desire for truth or truthfulness is a virtue, since to speak the truth is a good act, and when we act virtuously we become like unto what we love.

---

62. Hauerwas notes: "[T]he beauty of the liturgy cannot be separated from the goodness of the One worshiped; nor can the goodness of lives of virtue be devoid of the beauty endowed by the Holy Spirit. The lives formed through the liturgy must at once be beautiful and good, reflecting the beauty and goodness of such lives having an end not as some further accomplishment but constitutive of lives well lived." Hauerwas, *Performing the Faith*, 163.

63. Hauerwas, *Performing the Faith*, 163.

64. Robert Barron, *Bridging the Great Divide: Musings of a Post-Liberal, Post-Conservative Evangelical Catholic* (Lanham, MD: Rowman & Littlefield, 2004), 60.

And so the pursuit of truth or truthfulness in life and speech is an adventure in holiness and towards holiness."[65]

Our life and speech show forth the beauty of holiness to the extent that we are what we know and love and become what we do and say: listening to, learning from, and being led by the incarnate Word through whom all things have been spoken. "The Church exists, with all its human and material elements because God loves His creation, particularly his human creation, and communicates with us in our own language. What is more typical of the divine communication in human language than the Divine Word made man?"[66] *We speak because we have first been spoken.*

65. Joseph Incandella, "Similarities and Synergy: An Augustinian Reading of Aquinas and Wittgenstein," in *Grammar and Grace: Reformulations of Aquinas and Wittgenstein,* ed. Jeffrey Stout and Robert MacSwain (London: SCM Press, 2004), 30-31.

66. Charles Morerod, O.P., "John Paul II's Eccesiology and St. Thomas Aquinas," in *Nova et Vetera* 3, no. 3 (Summer 2005): 477.

The Grammar of the Preaching Life

✶ Grace of healing

H OW CAN listeners be confident that the women and men called to be "preachers" of the Word are capable of "speaking Christian"? Is it possible for a preacher to use the language of Christianity without speaking the "grammar" of Christ? In other words, can a preacher *use* the words of the Bible but fail to *communicate* the life of the incarnate Word? If the church's language is abstracted from its life as Christ's body, and the gospel is reduced to "subject matter" for "relevant" or "effective" sermons, has God's wisdom been conformed to human wisdom rather than human wisdom conformed to God's wisdom? And if Christian language enables us to see the world as it is, is it the task of preaching to transform Christian language to fit the world in the name of "relevance"? Or is it the purpose of preaching to conform speakers and listeners to the divine: human reality revealed by the incarnate Word signified by Christian speech?[1]

Alan Roxburgh describes what occurs when the identity of the church and its ministry are determined by pragmatic rather than theological criteria — and thus oriented by human rather than divine wisdom.

> The technical application of scientific rationalism assumed that it is possible to control life by manipulating our environment to achieve

---

1. Stanley Hauerwas, *Vision and Virtue: Essays in Christian Ethical Reflection* (Notre Dame, IN: University of Notre Dame Press, 1981), 46. I have paraphrased Hauerwas's words.

the ends we desire through specific techniques. With the right tools and skills it is always possible to get the job done. . . . Technology is the handmaiden of the anthropocentric church. It is not value neutral. . . . When training institutions equip leaders with a variety of techniques, the value system inherent in those techniques easily becomes the operational ecclesiology, defining the church's nature.[2]

Arguably, the most faithful measure of pastoral "effectiveness" in our time will be evinced by the virtue of practical wisdom that speaks appropriately to build up the church to be a truthful witness of the gospel through receptivity to the missions of the Word and Spirit, the *missio Dei*.[3] However, this will require the liberation of preachers and their preaching from captivity to modernity's dualistic "tyranny of the practical," which divides theology and practice into distinct realms of privatized faith and productive, technical reason, thus producing forms of "understanding seeking faith."[4]

2. Alex J. Roxburgh, "Missional Leadership: Equipping God's People for Mission," in Darell L. Guder, ed., *Missional Church: A Vision for the Sending of the Church in North America* (Grand Rapids: Eerdmans, 1998), 198. The self-study conducted by Willow Creek Community Church sheds much light on the challenges I am trying to outline in this chapter. Cf. Greg L. Hawkins and Cally Parkinson, *Reveal: Where Are You?* (Barrington, IL: Willow Creek Association, 2007). Although it is not mentioned by the authors of this study, what I believe the Willow Creek study clearly demonstrates is that when truth, beauty, and goodness no longer matter, the church — like everything and everyone else — is at the mercy of the market: the gospel is "whatever sells."

3. See Guder, ed., *Missional Church*; see also George R. Hunsberger and Craig Van Gelder, eds., *Between Gospel and Culture: The Emerging Mission in North America* (Grand Rapids: Eerdmans, 1996). David Bosch says: "Mission is understood as being derived from the very nature of God. It is thus put in the context of the doctrine of the Trinity, not of its ecclesiology or soteriology. The classical doctrine of the *missio Dei* as God the Father sending the Son, and God the Father and the Son sending the Spirit is expanded to include yet another movement: Father, Son, and Holy Spirit sending the church into the world" (quoted in Guder, *Missional Church*, 5).

4. See the extended discussions in Robert Barron, *The Priority of Christ: Toward a Postliberal Catholicity* (Grand Rapids: Brazos, 2007); William C. Placher, *The Domestication of Transcendence: How Modern Thinking about God Went Wrong* (Louisville: Westminster John Knox, 1996); Gavin D' Costa, *Theology in the Public Square: Church, Academy and Nation* (Oxford: Blackwell, 2005); and Brad J. Kallenberg, *Ethics as Grammar: Changing the Postmodern Subject* (Notre Dame, IN: University of Notre Dame Press, 2001). For the notion of "understanding desperately seeking faith," I am indebted to C. Clifton Black, "Augustinian Preaching and the Nurture of Chris-

Although it is admired by many for its pragmatic "effectiveness," this strategy imprisons speech within an autonomous realm of communication that is deeply inhospitable to the work of grace, the virtues and gifts of the Spirit, divine providence, and, ultimately, the joy of communion with God. In other words, a division of knowing and speaking in pursuit of "effectiveness" renders preaching theologically incoherent, reduced to a function of technology, or "will to power," in the illusion that reality is capable of mastery and control.

We will need a truly personal, relational, and embodied way of knowing and loving that participates in God's self-communication through the Word and Spirit if we are to imagine an alternative to what has been described as a "grammar of representation": those "modern and early modern tendencies toward skills of negotiating new products, new texts, and introduction of new technologies for organizing words and related *techne*, or craft, for realizing these texts."[5]

This description helps to illuminate tendencies within modern homiletical practice that have similarly affected the other theological disciplines. In the case of preaching, a "grammar of representation" is closely related to a "technology of Scripture," the "freezing of words" on the written page of "the text," which in recent years has appeared on the wide screen of the Power Point presentation. Yet on either the book or the screen, the "freezing of words" underwrites a privileging of mathematical accuracy and universal methods for arranging and transmitting knowledge, "a grammar of representation, which instantiates new dualisms, between reader and text, form and content, subject and object . . . and which [end] in Enlightenment deistic and theistic discourse."[6]

Such popular dualisms have contributed to a "hypostatization" of the sermon — the literalization of Scripture's words abstracted as "text" from liturgical and ecclesiastical use — which has helped to marginalize the church's participation in the truth of God's self-giving mediated through the apostolic witness to Christ. When the person and work of the preacher (homiletical character) is reduced to a technical, theologi-

---

tians," in *The Lectionary Commentary: Theological Exegesis for Sunday's Texts,* ed. Roger E. Van Harn, The Third Readings: The Gospels (Grand Rapids: Eerdmans, 2001), 607.

5. Peter M. Candler, Jr., *Theology, Rhetoric, Manuduction, or Reading Scripture Together on the Path to God* (Grand Rapids: Eerdmans, 2006), 13-14.

6. Candler, *Theology, Rhetoric, Manuduction,* 16.

cally neutral process (homiletical form), and separated from what is preached (homiletical content) and to whom it is preached (homiletical context) the discourse of preaching is redefined as atemporal, timeless "words about words" that "stand for" something else, that is, an event in the past, a "meaning" or "principle" behind the text, an experience within the listener, or the preacher's favorite program or agenda.

[margin handwritten note: Not giving a theological discourse]

Abstracted from particular things, people, places, and deeds, the language of preaching is easily detached from the concrete, contingent reality of the gospel, by which the Spirit graciously reorders the church's being and life to embody Christ's self-giving in the world. As Stephen Long says, "Knowledge is not an unmitigated good. Knowledge that should be bound by one social formation and its narratives of the good becomes demonic when it falls in the hands of another bound only by efficiency."[7]

Such forms of abstract "messaging" are typically shaped by the cultural norms and expectations of modernity and seen as the work of an "effective communicator" who may be more accurately described as a "Gnostic technician." In other words, popular forms of Christianity in North America, both "liberal" and "conservative," have assumed that being Christian means having a "personal relationship" with God, for which the church can be either instrumental or optional. This "privatization" of faith, when combined with technical reason, has more in common with ancient Gnosticism than its popular adherents are willing to acknowledge.[8]

The abstraction of the church's language, and thus its life, from the Trinitarian economy of grace contributes to a loss of coherence in hearing and speaking the Word and witnessing to the *missio Dei:* the creation and redemption of all things through the missions of the Son and Spirit. "Witness is constitutive of the character of what Christians believe. For the Christian witness to be truthful requires that Christians distrust all abstractions not disciplined by the Word that is Christ."[9]

---

7. D. Stephen Long, *The Goodness of God: Theology, the Church, and Social Order* (Grand Rapids: Brazos, 2001), 177.

8. See Stanley Hauerwas, "The Gospel and Cultural Formations," in *The State of the University: Academic Knowledges and the Knowledge of God* (Oxford: Blackwell, 2007), 39.

9. Hauerwas, "What Would a Christian University Look Like?" in *The State of the University,* 103.

When the Christian life (and thus the preaching life) is abstracted or "excarnated," as Charles Taylor has convincingly argued, from the "Word made flesh" — the exemplar and model of human being, life and speech — Christian language is rendered theologically and morally incoherent, because "there is no coherent language apart from a coherent community that does the talking."[10] As Paul Waddell argues, the life of Christian discipleship involves us in a steadfast commitment to "allow the Word we call Jesus to become the guiding grammar of our lives. . . . We are to speak to others in the language God has spoken to us; indeed, we are to become the Word that has been entrusted to us."[11] Hence the primary claim of this book: *We speak because we have first been spoken.*

Because God is the primary speaker and actor, witnessing *to* the gospel is inseparable from the transformation of a preacher to be a truthful witness *of* the gospel, by becoming a "partaker of the divine nature" through faith in Christ and the gracious empowerments of the Spirit that unite us to God through love (2 Pet. 1:4). Richard Lischer's comments underscore the importance of recovering an emphasis on the character and virtue of the preacher for homiletics. *[handwritten margin note: Final conclusion]*

> The person of the preacher is a good example of a topic that was of great importance for the medieval church but is now seldom discussed in homiletics. Most homiletic treatises from Augustine through the Middle Ages deal with the formation and holiness of the one appointed to preach. . . . Despite the interest in spirituality in both the church and popular culture today, however, one does not discern a revival of the classical preoccupation with the holiness of the preacher.[12]

---

10. Ephraim Radner, "To Desire Rightly," in *Nicene Christianity: The Future for a New Ecumenism,* ed. Christopher R. Seitz (Grand Rapids: Brazos, 2001), 219. For an extended narrative of Western Christendom, see Taylor's magisterial work, *A Secular Age* (Cambridge, MA: Harvard University Press, 2007), 613, where he defines excarnation as "the transfer of our bodily forms of ritual, worship, practice, so that it comes more and more to reside 'in the head.'"

11. Paul J. Waddell, *Becoming Friends: Worship, Justice, and the Practice of Christian Friendship* (Grand Rapids: Brazos, 2002), 22-23.

12. Richard Lischer, "Introduction," in *The Company of Preachers: Wisdom on Preaching, Augustine to the Present,* ed. Richard Lischer (Grand Rapids: Eerdmans, 2002), xiv.

The holiness of the preacher, moreover, is inseparable from the church's calling to be a holy people whose worship is the essence of living by receptivity to the self-giving of the Father in the Son through the Spirit's grace. This also assumes that homiletic excellence is inseparable from the truthfulness of a preacher's life, so that our habits of speech will need to be disciplined by the self-giving of the Father through the Son, in whom the Spirit makes us holy. In other words, prayer and preaching are inseparable. "All Christian speech is to be tested by the one work we have been given as God's creatures. We call that work 'liturgy,' which is the work of prayer."[13]

For theological reasons, then, the "grammar of the preaching life" is learned by participation in "a school of desire and wisdom that is concerned with both God and the world, and within which people can be formed in faith, hope and love . . . to live in the Spirit."[14] This is a way of knowing that is both deeply personal and public, so that the entire person is engaged with God and the world: the mind, the will, the imagination, the affections, and the body.[15]

Contrary to the talk of "relevance," "effectiveness," and what is "contemporary" that predominates in our time, the authority of the gospel — the saving wisdom revealed and enacted by the incarnate, crucified, and risen Christ — is made relevant, effective, and contemporary by the Spirit who instructs, delights, and transforms the church to know, speak, and do the truth in love. Mark McIntosh describes the intimate relationship between knowing, discerning, and loving in truth, or holiness:

> This love is the ground of the deepening steadfast knowledge of the neighbor, and sets flowing a renewable understanding of the other. We could even say that the divine loving inhabits the human relationship, making it possible and bringing to light within it the amiable truth of the other that God alone (sometimes) can know. It is precisely this feasting of the perception upon "the love of God in all its richness" that sets the mind free from fearful pre-occupations and

13. Hauerwas, "Carving Stone and Learning to Speak Christian," in *The State of the University,* 121.

14. David F. Ford, *Christian Wisdom: Desiring God and Learning in Love* (Cambridge, UK: Cambridge University Press, 2007), 225.

15. See Servais Pinckaers, O.P., *The Sources of Christian Ethics,* trans. Sr. Mary Thomas Noble, O.P. (Washington, DC: Catholic University Press, 1995), 11.

enmities, filling it with the divine guidance and so preparing the risk of the other — rather than merely the fantasized objectification of the other.[16]

Thus when the primary aim of preaching is effectiveness and utility — rather than speaking according to the truth revealed and enacted by Christ — it is easily corrupted to become idolatrous. For this reason, the cultivation of distinctively *Christian* speech requires attentiveness to the distinctive language of Scripture that incorporates us into the apostolic witness and unites us to Christ. As Robert Wilken observes, "Liturgy does not exist for the sake of humanity, but for the sake of God. If the Bible is the lexicon of Christian speech, then the liturgy is its grammar, a place to come to know and practice the Christian idiom and to be formed by it."[17]

Writing more than a century ago, Samuel Coleridge warned of the conditions that prevail when loving the truth of Christianity is made secondary to loving its utility. "He, who begins by loving Christianity, better than truth, will proceed by loving his own sect or church better than Christianity, and end in loving himself better than all."[18] Or as Karl Rahner once observed, "Christianity would cease to exist if it no longer had the courage to speak of the blessed uselessness of love for God; absolutely useless, since it would not be itself if man were to seek in it his own advantage . . . his own fulfillment."[19] And as Ludwig Wittgenstein says, "No one can speak truth; if he has still not mastered himself. . . . The truth can only be spoken by someone who is already at home in it; not by someone who still lives in falsehood and reaches out from falsehood towards truth on just one occasion."[20]

Learning the "grammar" of the preaching life will involve not only the transformation of speech itself but the lives of speakers; the sancti-

16. Mark McIntosh, "Faith, Reason, and the Mind of Christ," in *Reason and the Reasons of Faith,* 139.

17. Robert Louis Wilken, "The Church's Way of Speaking," *First Things* 155 (Aug./Sept. 2005): 31.

18. Quoted in Daniel W. Hardy, *God's Ways with the World: Thinking and Practising Christian Faith* (Edinburgh: T&T Clark, 1992), 190.

19. Quoted in Nicholas Lash, *The Beginning and End of 'Religion'* (Cambridge, UK: Cambridge University Press, 1996), 246.

20. Ludwig Wittgenstein, *Culture and Value,* ed. G. H. von Wright and Heikki Nyman, trans. Peter Winch (Oxford: Basil Blackwell, 1980), 35e.

fication of one's intellect, desire, and will through faith that comes by attentiveness to the Word through the Spirit's grace. "The 'faith' is not simply a set of doctrinal propositions, creedal affirmations, and moral codes. It is a world of discourse that comes to us in the language of a particular sort. . . . Language defines who we are; it molds how a people think, how they see the world, how they respond to persons and events, even how they feel."[21]

Because the Spirit evokes its own uniquely human response to the Word, neither the words nor the life of a preacher can ultimately be the determining factor in homiletic efficacy, or the preacher's "effectiveness." However, if the calling to be made participants in the divine nature is constituted by God's self-communicative speech, becoming a "preacher" will consist of becoming a person of prayer and virtue, capable of discerning the truthfulness of his or her life and words in loving acknowledgment of the Word who speaks creation and salvation.[22]

It is time to acknowledge what has become increasingly clear: the pragmatic use of homiletical methods and techniques, pursued as goals or ends *in themselves* and separated from knowing, loving, and enjoying God as the true end of all human activity and desire — that is to say, an impressive flair for public speaking, a "dynamic" personality and moving affect, a cutting-edge collection of downloaded sermons, popular video clips, entertaining illustrations and Power Point presentations, and the support of a technologically savvy, culturally attuned worship design team — cannot engender the kind of wise, experienced witness through which the Spirit works to form communities of faithful disciples for loving obedience to the Father in union with Christ.[23]

21. Wilken, "The Church's Way of Speaking," 27-28.

22. See Carver T. Yu, "Covenantal Rationality and the Healing of Reason," in *Reason and the Reasons of Faith,* 239.

23. See the insightful essay by Debra Dean Murphy, "Power Pointless: Video Screens in Worship," *The Christian Century* (July 25, 2006), 10-11: "The first question, then, is not how we can get rid of computers in worship, but, rather, whether we are paying sufficient attention to the ways in which computer technology in worship forms and shapes us. For if faithful Christian discipleship requires that we attend carefully to all aspects of our lives — that we reflect deeply and continually on how we are shaped by what we do (and don't do) — and if we're to resist the easy formulas and shallow pieties that distort and trivialize the church's witness in the world, then ongoing attention to what we do in worship (and how we do it) is vital to such discipleship."

Julian Hartt describes the church's calling as a living embodiment of the gospel for which the "preaching life" serves as obedient and exemplary witness.

> We have a great and desperate need for the gospel. The power of that word is not in utterance but in concrete life. The power of that word is that real, transcendently righteous and creative love. That alone is the power which can place us in solid and productive relationship to the real world. Hence, while the church has an utterance to make, sermons to preach, hymns to sing, and prayers to offer, above all it has a life to share. This life is God's free sharing of himself in Jesus Christ.[24]

And while this does not negate the place of skill, method, style, or other means in the craft of preaching, it does point to a fundamental need for cultivating the necessary wisdom and virtue to judge, discern, and order their use for speaking in ways appropriate to God's incarnate knowing and loving. It is in "[taking] every thought captive for obedience to Christ" that the Spirit conforms our intentions, desires, actions, and words to the Word who speaks creation and salvation. "Only when we affirm the glory of God in prayer and praise can the purpose of the human family be fully discerned, and thus the ethical criteria by which to judge the methods and contents of the various disciplines."[25]

Because the gift of the Word transcends human mastery and control, its reception will be inseparable from liturgical participation in the self-offering of the Son to the Father in the Spirit by which preacher and people are taken up into something larger than themselves: "Christ's own body, a body marked by God's triune giving and receiving."[26] We need an alternative to the excessive dependence on method, which serves to underwrite our strong desire to manage history in the name of expedience and effectiveness. On the contrary, we have been created for communion, for participation in the conversation of love between God and creation.[27]

24. Julian N. Hartt, *Toward a Theology of Evangelism* (Eugene, OR: Wipf and Stock; reprint, 2006), 117.

25. Gavin D'Costa, *Theology in the Public Square: Church, Academy and Nation* (Oxford: Blackwell, 2005), 190.

26. Elizabeth Newman, *Untamed Hospitality: Welcoming God and Other Strangers* (Grand Rapids: Brazos, 2006), 60.

27. See Chris K. Huebner, *A Precarious Place: Yoderian Explorations on Theology, Knowledge, and Identity* (Scottsdale, PA: Herald Press, 2006), 111.

Through the grace of the Holy Spirit the activity of the intellect, affections, and will are elevated and transformed by the outpouring of the divine goodness communicated in the Son. When preaching is practiced as a liturgical activity that springs from God's self-giving love, the person and words of a preacher are rendered good by the Spirit, whose grace orders human intentions, desires, actions, and words God-ward in conformity to Christ.[28]

Ellen Charry's insightful commentary regarding the task of theology in its various expressions (including preaching) provides a helpful way of characterizing what I have argued concerning the character of preaching and preachers: "[It is] the art of persuading people of the wisdom and goodness of God so that they may better understand God and themselves, and that they formulate what they do based on who we are as *homologs* [confessions, proclamations, or acts of praise and thanksgiving] of the Trinity."[29]

While taking seriously the full engagement of the preacher's humanity in the work of proclamation, "the Word of God resounds in, under and with the words of its messenger, without those words ceasing in consequence to be completely human."[30] My aim has been to press the question of how God's self-communicative activity through the incarnate Word and indwelling Spirit is allowed to be primary in preaching.[31]

28. L. Gregory Jones comments on the relationship between divine and human agency in speaking: "What is needed is a way of speaking of the prior action of God, namely the saving life, death, and resurrection of Jesus Christ, which also calls forth an account of the shape human activity is to take in response. Such an emphasis is found by recovering the relationship between being conformed to Christ and being called to imitate . . . or to pattern one's life in Christ. God befriends humanity in Jesus Christ, and in that gracious action, which originates in God alone, humanity is conformed to Christ independently of particular characters, virtues, and actions. Grace is the fundamental orientation of the Christian life. The context of this *conformitas Christi* is discovered in the salvation wrought by Christ. . . ." Jones, *Transformed Judgment: Toward a Trinitarian Account of the Moral Life* (Notre Dame, IN: University of Notre Dame Press, 1990), 110-11.

29. Ellen T. Charry, *By the Renewing of Your Minds: The Pastoral Function of Christian Doctrine* (Oxford: Oxford University Press, 1997), 149.

30. Jean-Jacques von Allmen, *Preaching and the Congregation,* trans. B. L. Nicholas (London: Lutterworth, 1962), 34.

31. In this connection, Frances Young observes: "Christian faith *(pistis)* involves trust based on convictions about the character of God demonstrated in his words and works. It involves the response of 'being persuaded' by God's communi-

The words of Saint Bonaventure, thirteenth-century master teacher and preacher of the Franciscan order, challenge us to recognize how a division of knowing and doing, content and form, life and being, is manifested in a number of ways, including

> . . . reading without repentance, knowledge without devotion, re-search without the impulse of wonder, prudence without the ability to surrender to joy, action divorced from religion, learning sundered from love, intelligence without humility, study unsustained by divine grace, thought without the wisdom inspired by God.[32]

Seen from this perspective, a recovery of the "grammar of the preaching life" calls us to an integrative way of being and knowing that involves rigorous study, prayerful devotion, and loving obedience in the conformity of our humanity to the "grammar" of Christ. And because the nature of this grammar is personal, participatory, and constitutive of the wisdom of love — rather than rules, methods, or techniques — it enrolls us in a school "whose pedagogy has the twofold purpose of weaning us from our idolatry and purifying our desire."[33] This training is best entered into as "a steady and endless enlarging of the heart through union in prayer and virtue with the Word, which is also a steady and endless growth in knowledge of the Father."[34] Thus nothing is more important for holiness than learning to speak and to use that speech to speak the truth to one another in love.[35]

Nicholas Lash describes the integral relationship between the incarnate Word and human authority:

---

cation, thus being led to conversion and conviction, assent to what seems the truth and decision to act in accordance with the will of the divine persuader. . . . So a preacher infected with the exuberance of God communicates not himself or herself, and yet the self is essentially bound up in the act of communication." Young, *Virtuoso Theology: The Bible and Interpretation* (Cleveland: Pilgrim, 1993), 131.

32. Cited in D'Costa, *Theology in the Public Square*, 218.

33. Nicholas Lash, *The Beginning and the End of 'Religion'* (Cambridge, UK: Cambridge University Press, 1996), 21.

34. Rowan Williams, *Arius, Heresy and Tradition* (London: Darton, Longman and Todd, 1987; quoted in Ford, *Christian Wisdom*, 238.

35. Stanley Hauerwas, *Sanctify Them in Truth: Holiness Exemplified* (Nashville: Abingdon, 1998), 61.

The God whom we traditionally confess as Christians is transcendent, wholly mysterious, wholly other: whom we confess as Father. But this same God has expressed himself concretely in our history, has become part of the form and meaning and texture of that history, as a man. Where the authority of truth is concerned, no man effectively exercises authority in respect of others unless he persuades, by the quality of his life, and character, and speech. The God whom we confess is a God whose self-expression as a man has convinced us, wooed us, compelled us to answering recognition, love, and trust. . . . [I]f we appeal too exclusively to external authority, then we shall be implicitly appealing to the authority of a God who is simply alien to our human experience, who simply contradicts it and stands over against it. Such a God is not the Father of our Lord Jesus Christ who has breathed his Spirit into our hearts.[36]

The liturgical language and action of the church engender the habit of constancy by which we offer ourselves and our words in receptivity to God's self-communication in Christ. Over time and through the Spirit's grace, we are transformed by listening, speaking, and acting in fitting ways for building up the church to exercise the necessary habits to believe, speak, and enact the truth of the gospel in the world. Speaking truthfully requires that we inhabit a world in which God dwells, speaks, and acts. Speaking of God cannot be reduced to saying things about God; rather, speaking of God will draw us into a relationship with God, in union with Christ, so that prayer and preaching are inseparable.[37]

By indwelling this scripturally illumined world through prayer, we are *habituated* into the "grammar" of a people whose life is continually renewed by Word and sacrament to be a sacrifice of thankful praise to God. Thus the "good sense" and "good taste" that attunes our ears, lips, and bodies to the mystery of Christ and the church, the "whole Christ," is cultivated by the renewing of our minds for speaking a "Word breathing forth Love."

David Ford describes the doctrine of the Trinity as "the most concentrated distillation of Christian wisdom," or the "grammar of God."

36. Nicholas Lash, *Voices of Authority* (Eugene, OR: Wipf and Stock; reprint, 2005), 11-12.

37. See Thomas G. Long, *Testimony: Talking Ourselves Into Being Christian* (San Francisco: Jossey-Bass, 2004), 11.

The Trinitarian "grammar" might be discerned in the narrative testimonies of scripture. Jesus' baptism has the Father acknowledging his Son as the Spirit comes upon him, and the baptismal formula in the final chapter of Matthew's Gospel is "in the name of the Father and of the Son and of the Holy Spirit." The resurrection is a "God-sized" event — the Father raising the Son in the power of the Spirit, the Son as the content of the Father's act, and the sharing of it and in it through the Spirit. The three climactic events of the death of Jesus, the resurrection of Jesus and Pentecost might be seen as having a similar grammar — the cross centered on the crucified Son, the resurrection as an act of the Father in raising the Son, and Pentecost on the outpouring of the Holy Spirit.[38]

Ford describes a Trinitarian grammar of Christian wisdom engendered by the Father's love, communicated through the wisdom of the Son, and inseparable from the Spirit's sanctification of the human heart, soul, mind, and body — which makes us holy: loving God for God's sake, and loving the people and world God loves.[39] Thus learning the "grammar of God" requires that preachers be formed by habits through the Spirit's grace in attentive receptivity to the Word of Christ through the church's prayer, praise, and proclamation.[40]

Andrew Moore has also argued that the grammar of Christian faith is learned by God's involvement in human life, that it is not primarily from theology that we learn how to use Christian discourse correctly, but from God's acting among his people through the Spirit of Jesus. Thus it is *God* who is the grammar of faith, since it is God in the person of Christ and power of the Spirit who teaches what cannot be learned from practices or rules. Doctrine, along with its interpretation as theology, is secondary to what it informs — that is, the church's performance of the gospel — which is alone its basis or foundation. However, there would be no Christian discourse without God's incarnate activity, because Christ is the one to whom Christian practices intend: "The material context of the grammar of faith is the presence of God in Christ. . . . The church bears faithful witness to God's language spoken in Christ by

---

38. Ford, *Christian Wisdom*, 210.

39. Ford, *Christian Wisdom*, 201-3.

40. See Daniel J. Treier, *Virtue and the Voice of God: Toward a Theology of Wisdom* (Grand Rapids: Eerdmans, 2006), 201.

the Spirit's declaring and enacting God's conforming of the world to his word according to the wisdom of Christ."[41]

Because the source and goal of the preaching life is knowledge of the Word incarnate in Jesus Christ it will commit us to both being and doing, to life and living a life, to speech and speaking.[42] In other words, the "grammar of the preaching life" describes a theologically formative "way of knowing" that is derived from, expressed by, and leads to knowing God as our truest end and happiness.

Prayer and worship create the most fitting ethos for sustaining the preaching life as a way of seeking the truth of the one whom we follow and proclaim.[43] "Such desire for truth or truthfulness is a virtue, since to speak the truth is a good act, and when we act virtuously we become like unto what we love. And so the pursuit of truth or truthfulness in life and speech is an adventure in holiness and towards holiness."[44]

The wisdom and holiness Jesus speaks and enacts — the full and final enfleshment of the Father's Word in the mission of the Son — is

---

41. Andrew Moore, *Realism and Christian Faith: God, Grammar, and Meaning* (Cambridge, UK: Cambridge University Press, 2003), 118-19.

42. Herbert McCabe, O.P., notes: "The center of the gospel is that in Jesus Yahweh communicates himself wholly to us. There are two fundamental things to be said about Jesus: one is that he is the word of Yahweh, the self-communication of God, the other is that he is the meaning of human history. . . . For this reason we can compare the coming of Jesus to the coming of a new language; and indeed, John does this: Jesus is the word, the language of God which comes to be a language for man." McCabe, *Law, Love and Language* (London/New York: Continuum, 2003), 126, 129.

43. Don E. Saliers observes: "Prayer is a logically required context for the utterance of theological truths. . . . This is a remark about the connections between the concept of truth and the activities in which speech about God is given religious force and sense. Christian beliefs about God and humankind function in a specific way of seeing. Such a way of seeing is acquired and sustained through learning to worship and to pray. It is precisely in the 'shaping' activities of prayer and worship that the language which asserts things about God and humanity has its natural home. If we are to understand what is claimed about God, ourselves, and the world, we must understand what it is to speak this way. If it is to bear truth, speaking about God must have a point in human life." Saliers, *The Soul in Paraphrase: Prayer and the Religious Affections* (New York: Seabury Press, 1980), 82. See also Saliers's insightful discussion, in the same volume, of praying and speaking the truth.

44. Joseph Incandella, "Similarities and Synergy: An Augustinian Reading of Aquinas and Wittgenstein," in *Grammar and Grace: Reformulations of Aquinas and Wittgenstein,* ed. Jeffrey Stout and Robert MacSwain (London: SCM Press, 2004), 30-31.

communicated by the Holy Spirit in liturgical readings and rereadings of Scripture by which the church is turned and returns to discern, love, speak, and live the truth that is Christ.

> The sanctification that characterizes those who are made disciples of Jesus through the work of the Spirit is that which makes it possible to see the world, which includes ourselves in the truth that is Christ. To receive such gifted truthfulness shatters our easy distinctions between that which is "spiritual" and that which is "ethical," between worship and ethics. . . . As creatures of a gracious God we should not be surprised to discover that learning to be truthful is an activity that leads us to acknowledge the one true God or that worship of such a God requires that we be truthful.[45]

Therefore, as a liturgical gift, disposition, and activity, the "preaching life" is learned through attentiveness to the Word, which evokes joyful praise to the Creator as the gracious source of our being, and to the one whom our being longs for and to whom it hopes to return in order to fully be. "Since it is in rendering the person of Christ, the living Word, that God is his own Word, the 'good things' in God's Word are God himself; moreover, we are the 'good things' we hear in the gospel, by attending to them with faith we are shaped to what we hear."[46] By following in the way of Jesus Christ, a preacher's whole way of being is transformed by the Spirit to become a "living sermon," moved and moving others to worship God in "the beauty of holiness."

Conformity to the shape of God's self-communication in Christ is thus integral to hearing and speaking the Word in ways that are faithful and fitting for particular times, places, and circumstances. Our ministries will need to be shaped by the wisdom or mind of Christ, hidden with him in God through incorporation into his death and resurrection, and re-created into "holy performances" of the Word. Without such conformity, which is derivative and participatory of God's prior revealing activity, all the skillful activity or sincere piety in the world

45. Stanley Hauerwas, *Sanctify Them in the Truth: Holiness Exemplified* (Nashville: Abingdon, 1998), 11.

46. Robert W. Jenson, "Luther's contemporary theological significance," in *The Cambridge Companion to Martin Luther,* ed. Donald K. McKim (Cambridge, UK: Cambridge University Press, 2003), 283.

cannot suffice for "one thing most necessary."[47] Holmer observes: "To know God requires that we become 'Godly.' . . . All of us can become Godly, and, once more, we know this because of the very grammar of God. This means that we can become one in heart, disposition, and mind with God."[48]

Saliers concludes: "We cannot show forth the ministry of Christ in the world unless we are first formed into his life, passion, death and resurrection — unless we comprehend in some way 'the breadth and length and height and depth' of the love of God in Jesus Christ."[49] He adds that theology begins and ends in prayer, that it "provides . . . a grammar for speaking and being in the world befitting who we are in God's love." Theology will therefore include a "grammar of the affections," a sensibility that is required for responding fully, even bodily, to the Word voiced in Scripture and enacted in worship. "The link between believing in God, knowing God, and the affections appropriate to the life of God, is the touchstone for all theological reflection. . . . Close-to-life theology which springs from the heart and speaks to it begins and ends in words and affections formed by the Word."[50] *We speak because we have first been spoken.*

47. Saliers, *Soul in Paraphrase*, 108-10.
48. Holmer, *Grammar of Faith*, 210.
49. Saliers, *Soul in Paraphrase*, 108.
50. Saliers, *Soul in Paraphrase*, 78-79.

Index